From Stanislavsky to Gorbachev

Russian and East European Studies in Aesthetics and the Philosophy of Culture

William H. Truitt
General Editor

Vol. 4

PETER LANG
New York • Washington, D.C./Baltimore • San Francisco
Bern • Frankfurt am Main • Berlin • Vienna • Paris

Douglas Graham Stenberg

From Stanislavsky to Gorbachev

The Theater-Studios of Leningrad

PETER LANG
New York • Washington, D.C./Baltimore • San Francisco
Bern • Frankfurt am Main • Berlin • Vienna • Paris

Library of Congress Cataloging-in-Publication Data

Stenberg, Douglas Graham.
 From Stanislavsky to Gorbachev: the theater-studios of Leningrad/
Douglas Graham Stenberg.
  p.   cm. — (Russian and East European studies in aesthetics and
the philosophy of culture; vol. 4)
 Includes bibliographical references.
 1. Studio theater—Russia (Federation)—Saint Petersburg—
History—20th century—Interviews. I. Title. II. Series: Russian and East
European studies in aesthetics and the philosophy of culture; v. 4.
PN2726.L4S74   792'.0947'453—dc20   93-34954
ISBN 0-8204-2285-1
ISSN 1065-9374

Die Deutsche Bibliothek-CIP-Einheitsaufnahme

Stenberg, Douglas Graham:
From Stanislavsky to Gorbachev: the theater-studios of Leningrad/Douglas
Graham Stenberg. - New York; San Francisco; Bern; Washington D.C./
Baltimore; Frankfurt am Main; Berlin; Wien; Paris: Lang.
 (Russian and East European studies in aesthetics and the philosophy of
 culture; Vol. 4)
 ISBN 0-8204-2285-1
NE: GT

Cover design by James F. Brisson.

The paper in this book meets the guidelines for permanence and durability of
the Committee on Production Guidelines for Book Longevity of the
Council on Library Resources.

© 1995 Peter Lang Publishing, Inc., New York

All rights reserved.
Reprint or reproduction, even partially, in all forms such as microfilm,
xerography, microfiche, microcard, and offset strictly prohibited.

Printed in the United States of America.

For my friends in Russia

Table of Contents

List of Photographs and Illustrations ix
Introduction 1

Part I. Interviews
Iurii Aleksandrovich Smirnov-Nesvitskii 8
Aleksandr Alekseevich Maslov 12
Tat'iana Andreevna Zhakovskaia 16
Lev Gennad'evich Sundstrem 20
Elena Viktorovna Markova 24
Akhmat Rashidovich Bairamkulov and
Alla Grigor'evna Minina 30
Vadim Zhuk 40
Marina Iur'evna Dmitrievskaia 46
Olga Kirsanova and Dmitrii Miropol'skii 50
K. N. Chernozemov 62
Maksim Maksimov 64
Vadim Gushchin 68
Isaak Romanovich Shtokband 72
Notes 78

Part II. Questionnaires
The Theater of the Absurd 92
Arena 94
The Leningrad Chamber Theater 97
Beyond the Black River 100
Da-Net 103
The Twelve 106
The Verb-Word 108
The Globe 111
The Leningrad Student Theater 114
The City 117
I and Thou 120
The Comedians 123
The Puppet 126
The Mummers 129
The Leningrad State Theater-Studio 132
The Mimegrants 135
The Mime Theater "Jester" 138
The Young Theater 141

The Bridge 143
The Theater-Studio on Lesnoi 146
The House of the People 149
Four Little Windows 152
The Theater of One Actor 155
The Theater-Studio of Pantomime 157
The Comedian's Refuge 160
The Theater of Real Art 163
St. Petersburg 166
7-77 169
The Kinematic Theater Sharmanka 172
The Dark Blue Bridge 175
Sabbath 178
Studio-87 182
Terra-Mobile 185
The House on Trinity Meadow 188
Time 191
The Theater Studios 194
The Crossroads 197

Part III. The Theater-Studios of Leningrad
The Theater-Studios of Leningrad:
Variety, Concert, Music, and Other Studios 202

Photographs and Illustrations 223
Bibliography 245
The Contributors 247

List of Photographs and Illustrations

Iurii Aleksandrovich Smirnov-Nesvitskii	224
Subbota	225
Aleksandr Alekseevich Maslov	226
Dom na Troitskom pole	227
Tat'iana Andreevna Zhakovskaia	228
Sharmanka	229
Lev Gennad'evich Sundstrem	230
Elena Viktorovna Markova and the Author	231
Akhmat Rashidovich Bairamkulov	232
Alla Grigor'evna Minina	233
Vadim Zhuk	234
Chetvertaia stena	235
Marina Iur'evna Dmitrievskaia (holding journal) with the Staff of *Predstavlenie*	236
Program from *We Play the King*	237
Vladimir Bogdanov, K. N. Chernozemov, and Evgenii Ganelin	238
Maksim Maksimov	239
Vadim Gushchin	240
Isaak Romanovich Shtokband	241
K. N. Chernozemov, Evgenii Ganelin, and Vladimir Bogdanov	242
Elena Viktorovna Markova and the Author	243

All portrait photographs courtesy of L. A. Kudinova. The photograph of Chetvertaia stena is also by L. A. Kudinova. German Pavlov took the promotional photograph of Dom na Troitskom pole provided by Aleksandr Maslov. Iurii Smirnov-Nesvitskii gave me the publicity photograph of Subbota. Photographs of Sharmanka and Irina Iakovleva (frontispiece) were provided by Tat'iana Zhakovskaia. The picture of Irina Kushnir (frontispiece) was taken by Iu. Bogatyrev.

Life's but a walking shadow, a poor player,
That struts and frets his hour upon the stage,
And then is heard no more. It is a tale
Told by an idiot, full of sound and fury,
Signifying nothing.
Macbeth

Be not afeard, the isle is full of noises,
Sounds, and sweet airs, that give delight and hurt not.
Sometimes a thousand twangling instruments
Will hum about mine ears; and sometime voices,
That if I then had wak'd after long sleep,
Will make me sleep again, and then in dreaming,
The clouds methought would open, and show riches
Ready to drop upon me, that when I wak'd
I cried to dream again.
                              The Tempest

Irina Kushnir

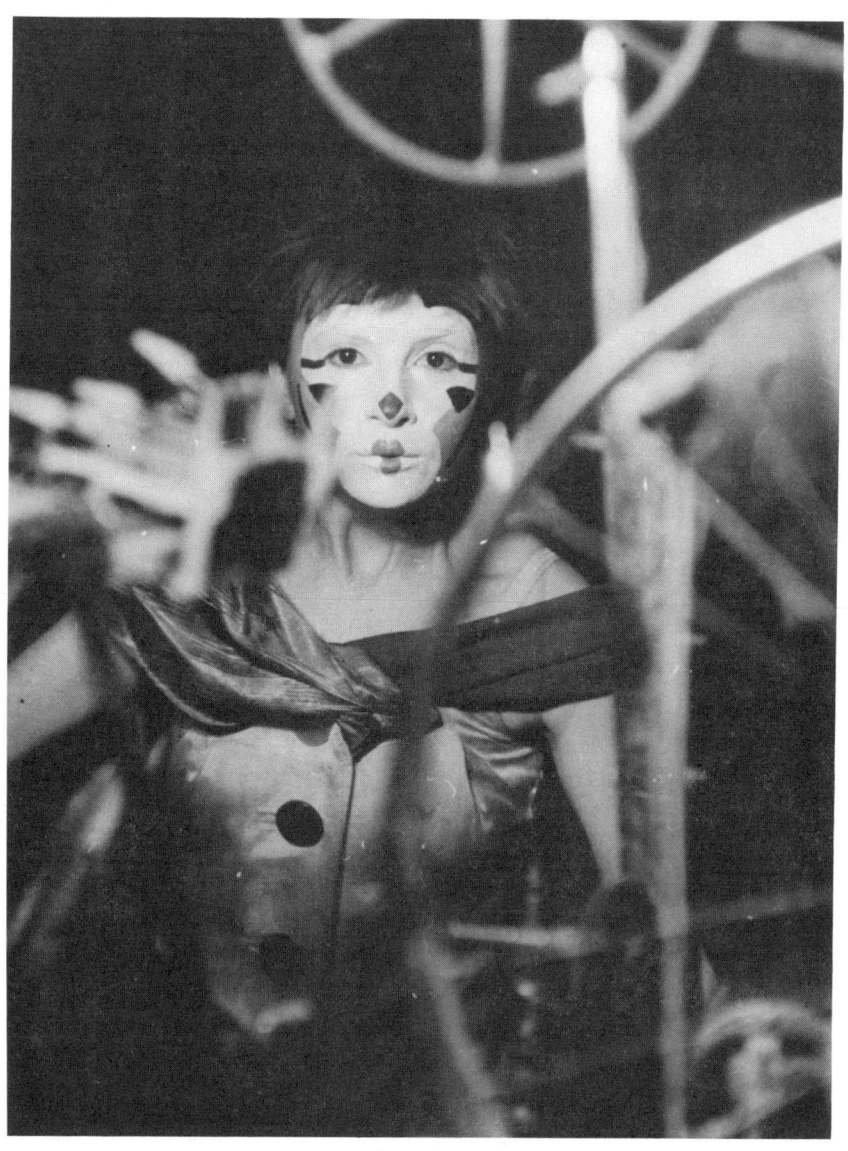

Irina Iakovleva of Sharmanka

Introduction

Despite certain rumblings in the atmosphere, I did not anticipate when I left Leningrad in July of 1991 that yet another Russian revolution was only weeks away. Then in August, while visiting my parents in Maine, I saw tanks rolling through Moscow on CNN. I could not know that my friend, Vadim Gushchin, had donned his army uniform, bid farewell to his tearful wife, and joined his fellow citizens on the barricades of what would again become St. Petersburg. Yet another friend and colleague, Marina Smyslova, received her visa from the American Consulate when the coup was unfolding, flew off to the United States from the Leningrad airport, and learned when she arrived at JFK that the plot had failed.

During the 1989-90 academic year, I studied the theater-studios of Leningrad as an American Council of Teachers of Russian Variable Term Scholar at the Herzen Institute. I interviewed directors, actors, and critics who were either associated with specific studios or familiar with the movement. In addition, the work involved the distribution of questionnaires to theater-studios identified by specialists from the Leningrad State Institute of Theater, Music, and Cinematography (LGITMiK). The openness with which respondents addressed both the artistic and social ramifications of the movement was impressive. I had been concerned about publishing this work and consulted with those whom I interviewed in that regard. Surely under Gorbachev such precautions seemed far less necessary. But the people with whom I worked were justifiably realistic about the future; with regard to totalitarian crackdowns on free speech and those who exercise that right, old habits die hard. The interviews and questionnaires, however, offer a glimpse of the studio life in Leningrad at the close of the Soviet era.

The results of the year were varied, long-lasting, and, at times, unexpected. More than the research itself, the greatest benefit was further bridgebuilding among educators and artists in Russia and the United States. Since 1981 I have maintained contact with members of what was the Theater on Krasnoi Presne in Moscow. This association resulted in the visit of the studio's artistic director, Iurii Zaitsev, to Colorado College on a Venture Grant during the spring of 1991. Vadim Gushchin, a professional actor from the Theater of Drama and Comedy, taught an innovative course in the fall of 1991 at the College, "Intensive Spoken Russian through Theater." His efforts were so well received that he was invited back for the spring of 1993.[1]

On yet another Venture Grant from Colorado College, Elena Markova of the St. Petersburg Institute of Theater, Music, and

Cinematography, lectured on mime in the spring of 1992. Her visit coincided with those of the artists, Natasha Fisson and Sergei Sherbin, who comprise the St. Petersburg Comic Trust. Both performed extensively during the Colorado Springs Imagination Celebration, sponsored by the Kennedy Center for the Performing Arts.[2] Ms. Fisson and Mr. Sherbin were assisted by Marina Smyslova, who has taught adjunct courses at Colorado College. Evgenii Ganelin and Vladimir Bogdanov, with whom I worked on bilingual Chekhov presentations, have since recorded their work for distribution throughout Europe, Australia, and the United States. They maintain active contacts with representatives from Columbia University. Such were some of the professional and cultural benefits from the year in Leningrad. But what of the studios themselves?

Ironically, many of the phenomena characteristic of Stanislavsky's[3] and Meierkhol'd's beginnings, as indicated in K. L. Rudnitskii's *Russkoe rezhisserskoe iskusstvo: 1898-1907* (*The Russian Art of Direction: 1898-1907*), have not faded with time. Concerns about foreign influences, conflicts between Moscow and St. Petersburg, the selection of actors, a changing interest in theater, the public's influence on repertoire, financial difficulties, and differences between professional and amateur theaters were just as relevant during 1989-90. It is precisely these kinds of questions that the theater people, educators, and critics were able to address.

The definition of a theater-studio and the movement's background are offered by Lev Sundstrem. He discusses the difficulty of identifying the legitimate studios which attempt to function as active working theaters. Vadim Gushchin, Aleksandr Maslov, and Tat'iana Zhakovskaia deal with the subject of an actor's training, especially when a younger artist attempts to tackle psychologically demanding roles. Understandable to any struggling actor are Akhmat Bairamkulov's views on the artist's life in Leningrad, a calling filled with hardship, struggle, and creative fulfillment. Candid assessments of the studios' artistic results are provided by Marina Dmitrievskaia. Elena Markova addresses such topics as the loss of art and audience, commercialization, financial concerns, and again, the artist's commitment to train and perform. Vadim Zhuk recalls his experiences with attempts at censorship, while the differences between amateur and professional theaters are examined by Aleksandr Smirnov-Nesvitskii of the established studio Subbota. Especially revealing are the comments of Olga Kirsanova and Dmitrii Miropol'skii, who chronicle the rise and decline of a studio through its all-too-common politics and maneuvering.

Overall characteristics of the movement are evident from the questionnaires answered by thirty-seven studios. For example, the repertoires of individual studios reveal both an appreciation of world theater and an emphasis on Russian themes and traditions. Yet a troupe must often perform popular children's shows several times a day, at the expense of other productions, in order to make ends meet. Performers are invariably young; few have formal theater training. Only a handful of studios have their own performance space. Rent demanded of the studios by the State-owned theaters is often much higher than the norm. Compensation for the actors, even by the standards of that time before today's hyper-inflation, is rarely adequate.[4] Ticket prices make the productions generally accessible, but many comment on the decline of an enthusiastic theater public. There are also problems with the distribution of tickets and advertising. In short, the documents portray struggles common to amateur theaters everywhere as well as conditions specific to artists functioning in the twilight of Soviet Leningrad.[5]

It was evident during discussions with those whom I interviewed that the Leningrad studio movement under Gorbachev echoed a long tradition. Solomon Tresser has compiled a list of 147 theater establishments from 1917-1945, and to the extent that the perestroika boom in theater-studios reflected a new openness in society, Tresser's data highlights several key periods of Soviet history. Of the theaters in his list for which specific dates of operation are provided, seventeen were in existence from 1917-20, ten which began after 1917 ceased to exist in the following decade, and sixty-nine functioned exclusively in the twenties.[6] Certainly the explosion was indicative of the society before Stalin consolidated his power. In this regard, consider that eight theaters which began in the twenties ceased to exist in the thirties and eleven theaters operated and closed in the thirties. Only one theater in both groups closed after 1937, as Stalin's Terror continued to claim the lives of millions. Of the eleven theaters that shut down during the forties, all ceased to function by 1941, the beginning of the Great Patriotic War with Nazi Germany. Such statistics reveal that the city's theater history, in many respects, mirrored political and historical events during torturous times.

As Akhmat Bairamkulov states, "Russia is made up of certain paradoxes." Indeed, the studio movement and Soviet theater in general can be better appreciated by acknowledging such paradoxes that pervaded art and society. Perhaps the best way to grasp the ironic underpinnings of the movement in 1989-90 is to consider two statements. The first was written a year before the invasion of Czechoslovakia. The second is attributed to Meierkhol'd.

> In the early fifties the Communist Party began resolutely to re-establish Leninist principles in all spheres of the country's social life, including theatrical art. The true method of socialist realism, allowing scope to artists of most varied individualities and affording freedom of creative

searchings, once again stimulated the development of Soviet theatre. The Soviet people's spiritual life acquired unprecedented intensity, their mental horizons broadened immensely and their cultural contacts with other nations of the world extended as never before. Marked progress was achieved in science, economics and culture within a very short time. All this could not but influence Soviet theatre.

The new productions of Vishnevsky's *Optimistic Tragedy* at the Pushkin Drama Theatre in Leningrad, of Mayakovsky's *Bath-House* and *Bedbug* at the Theatre of Satire in Moscow, and of Leo Tolstoy's *The Power of Darkness* at the Maly Theatre proved harbingers of the new theatrical spring.[7]

I am always surprised when it is necessary to read obituaries and various epitaphs about leading people whom I was fortunate to know personally. Is it they or not? Who says when reading elegiac pages about A. P. Chekhov, V. F. Komissarzhevskaia, A. Blok, and E. B. Vakhtangov that they were in life very happy people? But I remember this very well since I myself laughed together with them. I remember one day on tour in Poland when Komissarzhevskaia and I laughed all day over every trifle--such was the mood. I remember that Chekhov was almost always laughing. And when meeting, Vakhtangov and I cut up and cracked jokes more than discuss significant things in a penetrating way. Or perhaps I am such a flippant and careless person that they behaved themselves with me that way? I do not think so. If after my death you should read remembrances where I am depicted as a haughty priest due to my own sense of importance, uttering eternal truths, I instruct you to declare that this is all lies, that I was a happy person. First of all, because I love to work more than anything else, and it is joyful to work. Secondly, because, and this I firmly believe, when something is said as a joke, it is often far more serious than that which is expressed in earnest.[8]

Meierkhol'd was executed by Stalin's henchmen. He had been arrested the day after passionately expressing his ideas on the theater at a Moscow forum in June of 1939. Shortly thereafter his wife, the actress Zinaida Raikh, was savagely murdered in their home. The exact date of his death was revised by the Soviets over the years. And the obligatory bombast of the first statement seemed long gone by the time I began my work in the fall of 1989. Nevertheless, the movement did not flourish in an artistic and historical vacuum. At that time, artists struggled to find a voice in the city and were led by some who committed themselves to the theater long before Gorbachev's perestroika. The vagaries and threats of State politics were replaced with economic uncertainties and collective drives toward an unfettered art. It seemed to me that the best of the movement could never be measured in terms of a financial balance sheet.

Indeed many of its participants answered their calling with genuine sacrifice in a land where art was often respected more for the feelings it evokes than the monetary profits to be derived therefrom. All the same, many studios have become victims of changing economic conditions and demands.

In 1981, while studying at the Pushkin Institute in Moscow, I had the good fortune to see several productions at the Malaia Bronnaia Theater. The late director, Anatolii Efros,[9] was kind enough to provide me with tickets. He told me of his work at the Guthrie Theater in Minnesota. Before I left, I gave him some records by his favorite musician, Dave Brubeck. During a performance of Gogol's *Marriage*, the actor Durov was just finishing Zhevakin's monologue in which the suitor tries to understand his loneliness. Without a doubt, the text enables an actor to find tears through laughter. And the audience hushed as Durov shed a tear toward the end of his speech. That moment, more than any other during the fall, crystallized for me the wonderful opportunity to learn about the Russian culture and people. And certainly the miracles continued in Leningrad! I experienced an unforgettable rehearsal of *Crime and Punishment* at the House on Trinity Meadow, the freedom and linguistic range of *We Play the King*, Sergei Dreiden's one-man *Inspector General*, journeys toward magic and childhood in the Sharmanka studio, a very contemporary *Macbeth* at Subbota, Uncle Remus's tales, and the tragedy of Judas Iscariot. On and on.

As an American in Russia, I often felt that what I experienced and perceived could never be definitively understood or communicated through my Western sensibilities. There were so many qualities of feeling and spirit which hovered beyond my fingertips. In that regard I would prefer to let the artists, scholars, and critics, despite the difficulties associated with translation, speak for themselves. For many years they have helped keep the word alive through their work and commitment to Russia's culture. Hopefully, the results of this study will be of benefit to theater people in St. Petersburg and of value to others who are interested in the Russian theater tradition and Soviet theater at that time.

So many people gave of themselves in this undertaking. Iurii Zaitsev and Larisa Pavlovna Sontseva of Moscow were especially encouraging in the days when this project was only a dream. Later, Marina Smyslova, Elena Shalamova, Maria Semenova-Kingisepp, and Elizaveta Listova were extremely helpful with proofreading, translation questions, and transcriptions from tape recordings. Leonid Kessel'man was instrumental in helping to formulate and print the Russian questionnaires. I wish to thank Liudmila Alekseevna Korobova of STD for agreeing to receive completed questionnaires. Alma Law, Co-Editor of *Soviet and East*

European Performance and Omry Ronen of the University of Michigan provided help with specific points of translation and literary history respectively. Marino Deseilligny of the University of Washington gave me information regarding French theater history. I am very grateful to Kerry Williams of Bryn Mawr College for proofreading the text. Nataliia Shevchenko of Bryn Mawr proofread the English and Russian lists of studios. Zina Luft of Bryn Mawr looked over the Russian sections in the text. Nina Karp, Sim Ngo, and Mihaela Teodorescu helped with computer formatting at Bryn Mawr. Chris Unger of Kutztown University also assisted me with technical computer problems. I wish to thank Andrew M. Patterson and Judith E. Regueiro of Bryn Mawr's Canaday Library for their help with some specific reference questions. To Maria Naimark I am especially indebted for revising the list of studios. She also updated information on some theaters in that list during the summer of 1991. I am grateful to Heidi Burns of Peter Lang for believing in this work and to Kathy Iwasaki, also of Peter Lang, for her help with editing and production.

Alla Grigor'evna Minina and Akhmat Rashidovich Bairamkulov, formerly of Leningrad VOTM, provided tremendous support throughout the year. My experience in Leningrad could not have been as wonderful without the friendship of Vadim Gushchin, his wife Irina Kushnir, and their son Alesha. Tim O'Connor and Dan Davidson, both of the American Council of Teachers of Russian, created the opportunity to pursue this work through the Variable Term and Research Scholar programs. Ray Tharan's friendship has been invaluable. George Pahomov, as always, has been truly supportive. I am grateful to my parents, T. Douglas and Shirley Stenberg, and to my in-laws, Frode and Anne Nordhoy, for their love and support. I have been blessed with the love, thoughtfulness, wisdom, and kindness of my wife Kari. Finally, I am deeply grateful to Elena Viktorovna Markova, whose faith, counsel, and vision allowed me to gather the information contained herein. Whatever insights and useful material may be derived from the work are largely due to her guidance. As far as possible errors and omissions are concerned, they remain, despite my best efforts, exclusively my own.

PART I

INTERVIEWS

Iurii Aleksandrovich Smirnov-Nesvitskii
November 20, 1989
Subbota

Stenberg: Could you possibly describe the history of your theater. Or could you talk about the theater movement in Leningrad today? As you wish.

Smirnov-Nesvitskii: I will start with the movement. At present, the studio movement is organically entering the theater process in general. Both the traditional theaters (old and professional) and the new ones--they are working on one problem: how to bring back the audience. Because the ecology has been disturbed; that is how we describe "Violated Lake Baikal" or the poisoned air. It's the same thing. The audience has ceased to be theater-oriented, and even if they come to the theater, they look at a production as they would watch television, as a video, but they do not react emotionally as in the theater.

Stenberg: Who's guilty in this?

Smirnov-Nesvitskii: That which is guilty is the fact that for many years we drove the audience from the theater, politicizing it, offering these topics, these histories, which film and television and even literature convey with great success. But personally, the specific theater contact between the actor and the audience cannot be repeated; it has been lost. Thus, it is now necessary to bring the audience back to the theater and to again accustom this new generation to the idea that there is such an art form--the theater. It acts upon the audience differently from other arts and by means of a special specific form. And when Subbota arose,[10] we were then intuitively working on this very task. We wanted to create a theater of communication in order that there be contact. And today, despite the fact that things are very bad with regard to attendance, we are absolutely trying to carry on this goal.[11]

A production must be--and every representative of theater art has arrived at Grotowski's idea--he talked about the fact that each performance, in essence, is a meeting.[12] Stanislavsky arrived at the idea when they were performing *The Three Sisters*, and the audience had to sit in a circle with them and drink tea.

Stenberg: The family?

Smirnov-Nesvitskii: Yes, the family. And Brecht, even Brecht, who now is generally not very popular, he also came to the idea that if there is some kind of event on the street that this is already theater. The strength of theater is not that it shows some kinds of events or that it reflects some kinds of histories, but rather the performance itself, our very emotions, which are themselves events. The experience, the co-experience of audience and actor is important, not the idea. Therefore, Subbota has tried to ensure that the very people who enter the stage would be interesting enough to hold you or me for three hours. And the audience, perhaps, will leave and think, "But what was the idea all about?" But this is not important. What is important is that the spectator has spent three hours of his life (and already this is very great--human life is short--for three hours, this is also very important) either in joy or in tears. That is what Subbota essentially stands for.

But, if we are not speaking about our aesthetic programs, but about our self-supporting organizational programs, then Subbota is now advancing such a model. In my opinion, there is such a model in the West; now in Japan. I was telling you that Mikhail Vasserman also founded a similar small theater in Chicago where actors work for the soul rather than money. They earn money in the daytime, somewhere at other jobs. And only the service personnel [in the theater] receive money professionally: the director, artist, instructor, the lighting operator, the props person, and the others. But the actors do not work for money. What are we striving for by this? A theater does not need, as they have been saying here, forty to fifty people on the payroll. We need five to six salaried people on the payroll and then the theater becomes profitable. Profit (*rentabel'nost'*) means profit (*pribylnost'*).[13]

Stenberg: Understood.

Smirnov-Nesvitskii: This results in a small profit. We, in general, are a poor theater, but all the same, this allows us to live.

Stenberg: How is your theater different from professional theaters?

Smirnov-Nesvitskii: This is a difficult question, because after all we also have professional demands on the actors. In general, art either exists or it doesn't. A professional production or an unprofessional one does not happen. There must be art, and it is not important how it is created. Peter Brook said, "When an actor works in a professional theater, he quickly becomes tired, and for him the theater is a job." But for the unprofessional actor, to our understanding, the theater becomes an occasion for celebration. Each production is a festival, and we live according to the system of celebration. And thus we build everything from this, so that the actor desires to meet with the audience, with those with whom he is close. Thus the audience becomes a following like a sect around the theater. And this is a very good way, because by any other, the popular TV channel or the video-salon which draw many thousands of people, everything becomes the subject of an enormous mass interest. But here, we have a close circle of people. The first article about Subbota was in the newspaper *Smena*. It was called "In a Close Friendly Circle."

The discussion then involved upcoming *Macbeth* productions in Leningrad.

And here are our plans. We also want to stage Ostrovsky's *Talents and Admirers*. Our dramatist has such a play about how at the end of the last century, the merchants, the prosperous bourgeois, were buying the art of the theater, appropriating it. This is very contemporary for us when commercial interests have already seized art, keep it in their grasp, and torment a poor unhappy actress. This play is about the actress, about her talent, and about her admirers.

Stenberg: Have you worked in the theater a long time?

Smirnov-Nesvitskii: I myself, yes. I personally have dedicated my life to the profession of theater criticism. Right now I am in charge of the scholarly research section of art criticism at LGITMiK. I defended my doctoral dissertation on Mayakovsky. I have several books out--about Vakhtangov,[14] about Mayakovsky, and there is a small book about Subbota which came out in 1979. The fact is that I have commented [on the theater]. I went to the professional theaters, and then thought, it is better if I take these kids with guitars away from the gates [of buildings] and make this theater with them which each of us has in the soul. After all, each of us has his own theater in the soul. The kids and I got together twenty years ago and created such a theater, in order to be on to a good thing together.

Stenberg: Where is the theater going today, the theater movement?

Smirnov-Nesvitskii: Where is it going? Nobody is able to predict, just as it is unknown where the whole world is going and what will happen to us. But I think what's necessary is that Subbota, and perhaps the theater in general, become, as Vakhtangov said, a place where each person in the theater finds still another life,[15] a second life, completely unlike the one which takes place in reality--that the person may receive from the theater still another world. That is very important.

Stenberg: And what do you think, do the kids receive such a gift?

Smirnov-Nesvitskii: You know, it is difficult for me to judge, not based on how they behave--they are fanatics in this work--I feel that they receive an awful lot. There are scandals when a husband arrives and drags his wife out of here. But we try to remember that apart from the theater there is still a personal life, a family group, a type of commune. We often have weddings. They have their own children and we take them into Subbota.

We do not know where we are going, but most likely there, where all of humanity is going, to some kind of general establishment of connections between people. The reflection of all kinds of instincts which are rising very broadly towards peace, towards harmony, as in a church. All the same, the theater must remind us of something holy, as in a church.[16] Why do people come to a church, fall before an icon, and pray? Why is this not in the theater? Because people perceive the theater in such a way; it is possible to go, to be slightly amused, and yet it is possible not to go. The theater must become a necessity.

Stenberg: Do you think that passing through the period of stagnation helped?

Smirnov-Nesvitskii: It helped a lot. Well, you know that here an entire period has been called "the stagnation." It gave us an invaluable experience; how the theater can be isolated from the world and preserve all the best that people have. At that time they swore at us a lot, called us all kinds of names--that we were not taking part in our "tempestuous contemporary reality," that we were not taking part in five-year plans, that we were not supporting the slogans of the party, the slogans of the leadership.

Stenberg: They criticized writers in the nineteenth century with regard to the reality of contemporary problems and so forth.

Smirnov-Nesvitskii: Yes, you understand, it is very important to have some independence, to preserve some kind of personal view of things. This is very important.

Aleksandr Alekseevich Maslov
October 15, 1989
Dom na Troitskom pole

Maslov: Well, we have been together here for ten years, and for ten years we have attempted to construct some kinds of basic principles which I advocate. I have no kind of determined technology in order to manufacture an actor. The point is that today it is simply difficult to work according to that kind of plan when a person arrives with, all the same, a very distorted psychology. And the entire situation is to attempt to return his condition, his person. And then when he comes back to himself, he begins to feel that he is a person and faith returns to him, and those talents which exist within him are simply realized. Because he was not born without talent; some kind of determining circumstances make him unable to express himself and to be. That is why the most important task is to find those hindrances in a person which impede him from realizing himself as a person; and once he has come to the theater--that which hinders him as a creative person. That is the first thing.

The second thing that is important is what I talked about yesterday--truth. Because for me this is a sore subject and a very important question. The entire situation is such that when the audience comes to the theater, we want them to leave as you did today. Do you understand? And in order for them to leave that way, we, before all else, have to become that way. And when we become those kinds of people, then we can create the possibility that something will take place with them. And the entire situation is based on the need to attempt it. The audience exists in one social system, in certain social masks. It is completely enslaved in these masks. The audience has a state of mind and an entire expressive apparatus, their voice, their bodies are enslaved. Why? Because that is the means to preserve their lives; to adapt themselves to a determined means in order to survive. Creativity, that is uncovering, uncovering the self, to continually reveal. Do you understand? Not to be afraid to be the kind of person I am before others. This is the essence of truth. Then when something lets me down, subsumes me, then something can happen with me. Otherwise, as Blok said: "There will be beautiful trifles, though around empty souls."[17] The soul must be filled with a great inner content. And thus the first task which one wants to fulfill is the attempt to return them to themselves--who they essentially are. To provide the opportunity for them, having arrived, to become their very selves; because there is very little time for them to be their true selves. And then it is already possible to speak about some kind of work, about some kind of movement. And the most important thing for me is the culture, the ethics of our human relations. Because otherwise all the rest will be a lie. Because whatever grows depends on the soil. That is, if the soil is immoral and without truth, without faith, then everything but truth will grow on it. But if the soil will correspond to that truth, then on it flowers can simply appear, beautiful flowers and not weeds.

Stenberg: How does your theater differ from others?

Maslov: I do not know. It is very difficult for me to say, but the one thing I can say is . . . because I, unfortunately do not see a lot, because I work a lot and have not succeeded in seeing a lot [of other productions], but today I have the feeling of a kind of vanity, the striving somehow finally to come into view and to be, do you understand? All the more quickly and faster as now is the time of glasnost; to seize more quickly a piece of the pie, to come into being all the faster. And thus I feel that the atmosphere is just right. It seems to me today is the period of time, as never before, to dwell very deeply on this and to feel, like the roots which must feed us--they are torn away, do you understand? That is the very culture of the nineteenth century, our Russian culture, which, if you will forgive me, provided a stimulus to world culture; that is theater, painting, and music, after all we know quite a lot. And after all, all people in the West know Stanislavsky, Mikhail Chekhov. Why enumerate? We understand it all. But here we are today, and the most interesting thing is that all this culture is returning to us from the West which we lost, which we squandered. And the most important thing is to understand one's own, before all else, sense of nation, one's own culture, and to work on it. That is why such authors as Dostoevsky and Chekhov interest me, because that very wonderful literature is Russian and it is an eternal source. It is what I consider the most avant-garde theater, because they have always put the idea of the person first, and today the most avant-garde theater will be that where the person stands foremost. Because there is a lot around us and in this stream the person is falling, falling. Understand? He is disappearing, disappearing with the rhythm of life and everything. And the whole situation is still such that . . . what is important . . . I am trying to raise the dramatic actor. The concept of "drama" is disappearing from the stage; we are replacing it with an outer show as if that were drama. And this is very deeply connected with society, because dramatic action is that action which implies an act, which must be performed before my eyes, not that which will be talked about but which is performed and which cleanses me. Then something happens to me like Aristotle's catharsis. Do you understand? It is the deepest and most moral. And all this comes off in order that the action still imply the concept of choice. But today when our individual [person] is deprived of an understanding of an action and choice; then in coming here, it is difficult for him to have a command of the meaning of drama and action as in the theater. Thus the meaning of drama is replaced by external factors, and does not involve the person. Because it is here that the bulk of life immediately arises; simply the understanding that though "I am alive," I do not have the right to behave like this in my own life.

Stenberg: They [the young actors] must struggle with these deep ideas and so forth in Dostoevsky?

Maslov: Well, aside from Dostoevsky, it is very complicated for them now in the studio, because they exist in a determined social environment. People are attempting to construct another environment which makes creativity possible. This is already in conflict with the overall state of the world, and it is impossible not to enter into conflict with it. And they find the conflict within themselves, because two worlds have already arisen for them. The first that arises for them is that which they find when they get here, that is, the state of choice which did not exist before. It is very difficult to act completely. And it is absolutely necessary to lead them to this. But very deep and strong human actions are needed. Not everything succeeds, and it is still difficult. But I think that it will work out, because they really want it to. It will most likely be so. I hope so.

Stenberg: These kids do not want to leave?

Maslov: You understand. Yes. Here you asked a question with regard to an academic institution, where they receive dramatic training or the like. Do you understand the point? That person who begins to deeply investigate things here . . . what's important. The theater, as Jerzy Grotowski said, is a meeting. Here we had a meeting with you yesterday. Today a kind of contact has begun to come into being. And that is why the meeting is important, and then the contact. We give each other a kind of energy and with this energy we nourish each other. This is very important, the question of human development. And the question of the quality of human development--what it is and where it is directed. That's the essence. Therefore we still work with many kids in the studio on the level of a meeting, but with many, it is already on the level of a tangible contact. But this contact has taken place. This means we have already begun to nurture each other. It means that we will then be together. And my important task as a director is not to be a boss or a director. It is important to me that there be contact in the theater and that we go side by side. I am simply that person who at this given stage helps them to go and rise. Once you have risen, then you are independent. And then you are all the more interesting and will be all the more brilliantly clear. Thus, we must not be above somebody, but by that person's side. And this is independent of education and age. And then that person begins to be transformed, he begins to reflect. But this is difficult.

I do not know if I was able, somehow, to answer your questions.

Stenberg: Yes, yes.

Tat'iana Andreevna Zhakovskaia
February 16, 1990
Sharmanka

Stenberg: I have two questions. Describe, please, your theater. And after that, would it be possible to speak a little about the studio movement in Leningrad today?

Zhakovskaia: You mean this theater or Four Little Windows?

Stenberg: This one where we are now standing.

Zhakovskaia: This is a very strange, and in my opinion, unique theater which, as a matter of fact, was created without our participation. But the master craftsman[18] simply, the one you saw, after ten years of work in the underground--it is a very deep Leningrad underground--created the kinematic sculptures which I first saw several years ago. And it immediately seemed to me that this is theater. And after that it was by chance, because we simply searched for a location for the studio; our master craftsman had nowhere to work. As it turned out, this was unrealistic, and then the idea was born: let's make a theater and the studio will be there. Because the master craftsman himself, in general, is a person who is indifferent to publicity. But every week up to ten people, about half of whom were foreigners, came to his room to look at everything. This interested them more. And completely by chance a location turned up for us, the one which we found after a year of searching (it is very difficult right now in Leningrad). It turned out to be quite large. We are the only theater-studio in Leningrad which received its own location. This is an absolute miracle, and I attribute it only to the karma of our master craftsman. Our being here is luck.

But this theater, when it was still at our master craftsman's house, was still a home theater which actors from my theater-studio, Four Little Windows, helped to make. I have worked there for twelve years, and basically, all the kids who came to this collective when they were very young have worked there from five to ten years. They are jacks-of-all-trades and have provided technical help. And then, when the location turned out to be so big, the question arose as to whether they, living actors, can work with the sculptures. And I began to realize my dream which I had had since my youth, because at that time I had some very good teachers, and the most important of them was Boris Osipovich Ponizovskii, the leader of the Leningrad underground. He was a brilliant theoretician, and instead of a theater institute, I, truthfully, preferred to spend time at his home. And so at that time he (when everything was unknown to us) inspired me with the theater of the pure actor . . . because it is a very dangerous game for the living actor who attempts to identify himself with an image. As soon as we cross to some kinds of depths in the sphere of the subconscious, it is fraught with such things that a person can land in a psychiatric clinic. All the pure truth which interests us is found in that realm which is already dangerous. And it is necessary either, as Grotowski, to have excellent training which provides the technique for safety, or what is needed is the ability to make things strange through a mask or doll.[19]

I had yet another teacher. He is still alive. This is Evgenii L'vovich Shifers; he is a famous person, the first among the Pleiad of the young Leningrad producers of the sixties. He was expelled everywhere, first from producing, then from film producing, then from literature. As a result he, a theologian and theoretician, lives in Moscow, and his articles are published abroad. It seems to me that this is a powerful theoretician, a person who converses internally with Florensky.[20] Yes, [someone] on that level. And in general, he considers the archetype of Russian theater to be the monk performing with puppets. Moreover with wooden, immobile, flat, conventional puppets; that is, not with those which are pulled by strings and resemble human beings. Thus the center of the medium is outside the actor and not inside his psyche. He is outside of it. And therefore he is already able to move out of the limits of his "I" and is open to meet the city, the world. Because, it seems to me, the death-dealing situation itself of the twentieth century is the person inside of himself.

I ran into this head-on in the studio four years ago when we put on *Hamlet*. I consider myself guilty, because this fellow performed wonderfully while I forced him to peer into those depths for which he was not ready. But being neighbors with these puppets gave us completely different possibilities. That is, we succeeded in building this theater. This is a miracle, because it is a very complicated situation at the moment when everything is disappearing. And the building materials are a problem, and the wiring is a problem, and we don't understand very well how we will exist further in these conditions. I am afraid that the only means to preserve everything--this is the customary psychology of Russia--is for someone to show something in the West. They will say something there, and then here they begin to respect and protect [it]. Because right now if a new staff of the RAIISPOLKOM[21] refuses to help us, we will not be able to exist, even with a full house, because this theater cannot pay for itself. It exists thanks to the fact that the chairman of the RAIISPOLKOM, that is the mayor of this district, wanted very much to be selected for another term and he therefore deposited 100,000 rubles. This is the only theater in the city which the authorities have helped.

Stenberg: Will they continue the support?

Zhakovskaia: It is not known. Very soon there will be a new mayor of the city, a new mayor of the RAIISPOLKOM. Even if they want to continue, they will simply have no money. They receive nothing. They have nothing, really nothing, and I know this. They have no means, they are powerless, that is, the country has ceased to be governed. They wasted an enormous amount of strength in order to build this. The chairman of the RAIISPOLKOM personally furnished the materials. This is impossible. It is simply economically impossible, because we must earn 2000 a month, but the rent of the location amounts to 4000 a year, that is, we must pay somewhere from 400 to 500 rubles a month for the location, and the kids receive the lowest pay imaginable while they do everything. They are the actors, the electricians, the radio operators, but it is impossible to raise their pay, because right now is not a time for the theater. People can pay eight rubles for a rock group (and sometimes twenty-five), but a children's ticket costs one ruble and two rubles for an adult, and it seems to them that this is already expensive. It is a very complicated time in general; people are just not concerned about the theater right now. I think that this actually is an adult production, but no one is going to adult productions in the city. And this is it--the main problem in the studio movement right now--while during the years of stagnation, as we call them, this movement flourished.

And here is the paradox. Right now the amateur movement of the theater-studios is doomed. For it will go either this way or that until the situation in the country is settled. In the previous epoch, an entire generation of directors and writers was wiped out. A writer sits, writes, places [the document] in a desk and in twenty years publishes it. But a director cannot do this. And thus the generation a little older than mine-- these are people who were not preserved. They were destroyed. They had no work and they lost their profession. They had no work, saw nothing, could not feed themselves, and did not know anything. Only now have we begun to publish Grotowski, whom the whole world has known for twenty years, and we have turned out to be relics of the insane period; moreover, and this is most offensive, of our past, our own ideas. Therefore we basically have not known our own theater for twenty-thirty years. Only now are we beginning to devote ourselves to it. We have had the rupture of the national culture. And now, the people have broken away from the [idea] that in general the arts are needed, that the theater is necessary.

What are they looking for? Amusements, pornographic films, and those about judo and kung fu have been allowed. Everyone is going there. And the period must pass before people will again want to dive into the depths. This is a very difficult period, and I do not know how many years are necessary. Right now it is a burned-out wilderness. Nothing will be able to grow in it for still another ten years. There is simply nowhere.

Lev Gennad'evich Sundstrem
September 21, 1989
LGITMiK

Sundstrem: Study was conducted at a main theater; these were young collectives, oriented towards an understanding of Stanislavsky's method,[22] which he brought forth. The theater-studios (studio means instruction) from the first were based on study or theater training.[23] Those studios formed on this basis sometimes became theaters and sometimes did not, and it is necessary to read about this. We will not discuss this in detail now. The Vakhtangov Theater was formed in this way, the theater which Stanislavsky organized into a studio at the Moscow Art Theater.[24] It later grew into an independent collective and became the Vakhtangov Theater.[25] Today it is the Vakhtangov Theater. This direction is understood. There was a kind of idea, a desire to attract the youth to theater ideas. The theater-studio as a study and assimilation of these ideas received further creative development, and the enrichment of ideas created the theater. That is how it is possible to explain the theater-studios in the first decade and in the twenties, before and after the Revolution. Then as you know, we have a history which is not simple, we had a time of quotas and cruelty, and there were no theater-studios. If there is learning, then it is only academic. If there is a theater, then it is a State theater and nothing more.

Stenberg: During Stalin's time?

Sundstrem: Yes, with Stalin. After the Twentieth Party Congress which we now call "the thaw," when we first openly acknowledged the cult of personality, certain independent sprouts of the artistic movement appeared, among which were theaters. The Sovremennik[26] was earlier a theater-studio. And it also grew from its origins of theater training. It was a program and then gradually became a theater. The term *teatr-studiia* was included in the theater's name. But it did not differ from other theaters in the way it was organized and managed. But the word *teatr-studiia* implied that young people wanted to bring forth fresh ideas which are based on certain traditions of the Russian theater but are still their own new ideas.

But today the word itself has lost its original meaning and can mean anything you want. Beginning with amateur collectives, who have no pretensions of becoming professional theaters, and ending with the complete professional collectives, which prefer the name theater-studio, we have today a number of organized exceptions which function as State theaters and studio theaters. Here there is the possibility of independent organization and activities based on other freer principles, although they are more complicated, because there is no government financial support. And today so much falls under the term "theater-studio" that it often does not have anything do to with a theater. A group uses the name theater-studio because then "we will be able to have this, this, this, and this, and therefore let's call ourselves a theater-studio." We have today concert collectives, pop-groups, which have a minimum of theatrical integrity, and if there were no need to make use of the economic benefits, these pop-groups would not call themselves theater-studios. What kind of theater-studio is it? It is a pop-group. But if it did not call itself a theater-studio, it would be difficult for it to function in our concert system. And when it became possible for them to call themselves a theater-studio, when the regulations appeared,[27] they received a variety of rights--financial, that is payment of labor costs, and so forth. Therefore, among those who today call themselves theater-studios, there are real theaters which are searching, as distinct from other theaters. As a rule, this process is not usually bound to a definite idea which makes the group distinct. Rather, it becomes independently organized. That very Kurginian, which you mention here in the text. Beliakovich is just the same. A person supports an idea, gathers a collective, and calls it a theater-studio. This is a different type of theater-studio compared with those during 1910-20 in Russia and then in the Soviet Union. And this is the thing that must be essentially understood.

Stenberg: How many of the original pure studios are there in the Soviet Union?

Sundstrem: Nobody knows. And I will explain to you why right now. Our government statistics functioned simply and comfortably until recently with regard to the theater, and not only in this area. Because we have over six hundred State theaters in the country, beginning with the smallest puppet theaters and ending with the Bolshoi. I do not remember at this moment the exact number, but it's about 650. And until recently there were no other collectives. All the theaters are State-controlled; they answer for each move or step they take and each step is entered in the accounts. First of all, there is the opening of a theater itself. No one was able to simply take a theater and open it. This was the decision of the Ministry and there were long-term plans in which the year of the opening was entered in this town or that, depending on what money would be available for it. And so forth. The development of this theater network and every step of this theater, how much of a profit it earned, the attendance, was calculated quarterly (every three months) in a year. These calculations were gathered and became the general statistics. Therefore, we knew how many theaters we had, how many productions they put on, and how many people attended and so forth.

Today they . . . and I talked about this at the Ministry, today the situation is strange. Our Committee of State Statistics publishes a report. For example, in the 1988 report it is written that there are this many professional theaters attended by this many spectators. But this does not apply to today, because earlier there were no other professional theaters. And now from among all this variety of theater-studios, amateur theaters have appeared which sometimes receive money and sometimes not. But we cannot call them professional theaters. But at the same time, among these theater-studios there are some which, according to their activities, are in no way different from professional theaters. Actors also work there who receive pay. That is, they are professionals. Among them there are many with a specialized theater education, and thus their theaters are professional. But the statistics do not reflect their number. This is an unusual situation for the State. Everything was stable earlier. I wrote an article in a theater magazine and tried to find an example of some kind of theater which ceased to exist, that is, one that closed. I found only one case. In 1968 one insignificant theater was closed, but nevertheless it was joined with another theater, and in the place of the two, there appeared one joint theater. And there were no other incidents of theater closings. All other theaters that were established were registered according to the plan.

But it's not the same with the theater-studios. A group has gathered. Someone accounts for it. But according to today's situation, they may go to the ISPOLKOM, be registered, and start working. But this does not mean that after two months nothing has happened with them. They have had words and have shut down. And now this is part of the system, because many registered theater-studios have come to the stable State theaters and this large network. The system is alive. Some theater appears, another disappears, and then again comes to life, et cetera, et cetera.

Stenberg: As in nature?

Sundstrem: This is normal. But our government statistics, to the extent that they were oriented on reports, were in need of reconstruction; this is the expression [perestroika] now in vogue. That is, one should only work according to reports. Now the theater-studios must work according to selective research, representatively, in order to characterize this or that, quantitatively, as a phenomenon in our life.

But they are not yet able to do this. Today, a theater-studio which is created in one of the regions of Leningrad, for example, is registered in the District ISPOLKOM. The theater gives a report to this ISPOLKOM, a declaration of the revenue, and nobody knows anything else about this studio. Therefore, no one can accurately identify the number of theater-studios in the Soviet Union at the present time. Even if one could say how many exist, it would be the same as saying how much fruit is in a basket, when there are apples, pears, plums--that is, the theater-studios are varied. In fact, it would be senseless to attempt to number them. And on the other hand, there is no system today to account for these processes.

A group was formed in the Leningrad STD[28] which gives organizational assistance to the theater-studios, that is, these theater-studios themselves gathered at STD and organized their own council. And a Party member is there who helps them in terms of organization. And today in STD there will be authentic information about what's happening in Leningrad.

We have a department of theater management. Last year one of our students wrote a senior thesis in which she analyzed the work of several theater-studios and attempted to identify all the theater-studios which now exist in Leningrad.[29] But among all of those identified, there are a lot of pop groups which I have already told you about. But in fact, this is not a list of the theater-studios. But it's impressive anyway. The last number in the list of theater-studios is 166. But again, to emphasize, it is very difficult to identify the type of theater according to its name. For example, the theater-studio Pantomime, headed by Efimov, is understood to be a pantomime theater. But if we consider the theater-studio Balloon, headed by Vetkin, then I must associate it with its name or what is concealed behind the name "Balloon." Either some theater activity, or a pop group, which is hiding behind the title of theater-studio. And this is a problem. And it will certainly be difficult for you.

Among those which are considered to be a theater-studio is the rock group Folk. It is written that it is a rock group, but in fact it has taken the status of a theater-studio; it is clear from what is written. But often it is impossible to understand what they are.

Here organizational questions are examined. The information is interesting, it may be useful to you, and you may have a look.

Elena Viktorovna Markova
December 6, 1989
ul. Lakhtinskaia

Markova: The situation with the theater-studios, of course, is very complicated, because from the very beginning it was not a uniform phenomenon. That is, this is not some kind of artistic movement which is winning a place for itself. There are people with various interests who practically and formally are united by this word "theater-studio." They all want different things. And they have, many have, of course, very different points of departure, not only in terms of art, but [different] human and economic stands and so forth.

What is the first thing, as it seems to me, which complicates this situation? For very many decades there was no possibility to open new theater organizations in Leningrad. Despite the fact that the city was already very large, little more than ten theaters existed in it. They were all located in the center. The peripheral outer regions were in general devoid of any kind of theater culture. And what is most important, these so-called State theaters did not have the right to die, which must not be the case with the theater. You will agree, it has a definite creative period and naturally, in order not to discredit the theater, sooner or later, having played its role, must give up its place to others. So that very right to die was closed. And if a theater was created, then it was forever, for a century. It became immortal and at once ceased to be alive.

Now, the possibility which has appeared is, most likely for today, the greatest achievement in all of these undertakings. Now, at present it is possible for theaters to be born, live, and die. True, right here, and already I do not know whether it is because of a strong feeling of indignation or something which has just come to me, but we did not receive this right as all normal people would, but only after Moscow.[30] It has already been a year in Moscow, that is, the second season that the theater-studios have functioned fully, but in Leningrad the question was still being decided. But if we return to the beginning of this problem, why it was impossible for us to open new theaters, it was due to the fact that the majority of directors--professional and very talented directors--left the city. And then the actors began to follow them.

Stenberg: Who, for example?

Markova: Oh, there are very many. It began with Shifers. Evgenii Shifers, Ar'e, very many graduates of Tovstonogov[31] (because there was no other move open to them), Kama Ginkas, Geta Ianovskaia, who now is the head director of the Theater of Young Spectators in Moscow. Very many, in general, left the theater for television or nowhere.

Stenberg: And the majority left for Moscow?

Markova: Both for Moscow and farther. And to your parts also. The city was literally emaciated, because it endlessly gave birth to talents, but they did not find the possibilities for the realization [of them]. A complicated process began here. Directors not only found themselves in this situation, but very many actors as well. Most likely, a lot of people have already told you that the organic, natural studio movement in Leningrad began long ago. It was possible to organize these studios much earlier than the appearance of the regulations.

Stenberg: Subbota, for example.

Markova: For example, Subbota, but it was still much earlier. The first sign, when a theater opened in Leningrad after a long break, was the theater of Malyshchitskii, the Molodezhnyi, which now is located on the Fontanka. It existed for a long time as an amateur student studio. Of course, it did not exist in the same way as a professional theater, not in those conditions, but a creative search was conducted there. They put on different things than the official theaters and created a new means of existence--sometimes from a creative impulse--sometimes from desperation, when there was no money for decorations. And the most important thing is that an intense thought process was going on there. Malyshchitskii himself is a professional director. And Geta Ianovskaia was doing the same thing for many years. She led an independent studio for many years here in Leningrad. Without any hope for success, it went along simply as a complete and utter existentialism. From time to time she staged productions in the professional theaters. But this was always a different group; it was always a valid undertaking which never was able to become a regular entity and, of course, every now and then there was success. And at present, when this process has been legalized, as it were, practically nothing of that strength has remained. But imagine, not to stage any productions for twenty years. And of course, a feeling of dissatisfaction remains with you, and up to the present time while you still have not realized it all somehow, it is difficult to go on. And now many theaters which are headed by the generation of people who for twenty years simply did not have the right to work, they only have succeeded in turning into mature men from young and talented people. But all the same, they still walk about in boys' shorts, because they still have too few productions behind them (behind the shoulders) in Leningrad in any case. They, of course, traveled to the provinces to stage [plays], but that, of course, is not the [desired] path, you understand. And at present, before setting off further to launch some kinds of new creative steps, they, of course, must have an opportunity to perform.

So the process goes on as the theater is catching up to itself. Moreover, a very significant coincidence is arising at the moment, when both creative and economic questions and problems are being laid on top of each other. Of course, now they are in very tough straits (scissors). The audience must pay a lot now (for the natural attempts of the theater to catch up with itself), because in order for the theater-studios to survive, they must be subsidized by the government, and it is very difficult for them in that they are not used to it and have no primary capital. They must [do this] at the audience's expense. But it's not the case that they come out to the audience and say, "Dear Comrade-Spectators, we have this artistic program. Can anybody help us?" And some kind of patron (Maecenas) will be found. And with today's inflation, I do not think that anyone will be found to invest money in an unknown venture when suddenly people can only promise to be talented.

So, then, what do they do? They have no other way out. Very often they do a production on a commercial basis and begin to exploit it mercilessly. Of course, there are those among them who have a conscience, who try not to perform this production frequently but on tour or in a rural area in the provinces, which, of course, is profoundly swinish because this is also not culture. But how, with some kind of noble goal, does one accumulate the primary capital in order to get settled, find some kind of rhythm in life--somewhere in the future, and not today, sometime, again sometime, but not today, not right now--to have the possibility for creativity, because no kind of creativity is possible without the material base.

During the last years I have been recalling the example of Stanislavsky all the time. When I was conducting excursions throughout the Theater Museum, I always told visitors that the Moscow Art Theater was founded by three people. Several who were more cultured were very surprised, because it has always been called (the theater) of Stanislavsky and Nemirovich-Danchenko. But we will agree. What if, incidentally, there had been no Savva Morozov, the factory owner, who greatly subsidized them? And if there had been no Stanislavsky and Nemirovich-Danchenko with their personal capital, then their artistic talents would hardly have been revealed so well. And this is the problem that has remained unsolved for our theater-studios today. They move toward various contrivances, and in no way do I fault them, you understand. A different process worries me, because now, having received the possibility to expand the culture and to place it on a new level, what we are doing is still unknown. Are we not destroying it further?

Side by side with these studios, which are attempting to catch up with themselves, the time has slipped away to make up for it and to find a new aesthetic, some aspects of which are the most interesting, although they are profoundly uninteresting to the audience. Therefore, I, for example, stand up for VOTM[32] with all my soul. Those studios are there which concentrate on finding a new aesthetic language. And this is a non-commercial variant. It is interesting for a tight circle of specialists, for theater people. Only they are able to value it, especially because it is very difficult to do a grandiose production at once; the experience takes place gradually. Thus, for example, the appearance of VOTM, although it also arose later in Leningrad than in Moscow (and only then in Leningrad); all our personal, organic demands for these or those forms, which are identical to our situation, were never realized until this time.

Why do I single out VOTM? It is impartial. STD took upon itself the responsibility of a certain sponsorship. It is possible there [at VOTM] to do a non-commercial production which will not be performed in a large auditorium, because without this endless experimentation (which interests no one except the drama-lovers themselves but which provides a new quality) the business will not move ahead, of course. There are quite a few atypical situations. For example, the theater-studio The Road[33] is suffering morally a great deal, because they are a theater without status; and you and I were there in a nearly empty hall, despite the fact that all the tickets were sold. That means that the organization of propaganda for the theater-studios is loathsome right now. Tickets are sold for Valerii Leont'ev [a popular variety show singer] and are dumped en masse for an unknown theater-studio. Of course, the audience does not go to it. What is more, whatever money they receive is nevertheless very offensive to the artist. Your performance is sold-out, but there are no living people, no eyes in the hall. This is horrible. It is difficult to perform a play in such conditions. It beats so strongly against the spiritual potential and saps [one's] energy.

Stenberg: And they perform?

Markova: Yes, of course, they perform. But there is still a typical situation with their favorite play. For all that, they are compelled to perform commercial plays. What worries me a great deal is the fact that the commercial plays are done right now due to the deficit of children's productions. We had some statistics, if I am not mistaken, that there are very few. A Leningrad child on average can attend one production a year, and this is not every child. It was really a very large deficit in the recent past. Take a look right now at the repertoire of the theater-studios: they are full of children's productions and they pay for themselves. But of course, the level and the quality of the production are important here. And it cannot be high, because they must perform at random performance spaces--schools, very often on unadaptable stages, without wings and lighting. That is, no kind of magic in a play is being fostered in children. In this way, we are not cultivating a new theater public, a new generation. This is the best opportunity to train for the theater, as it is for television. It is possible to watch cartoons when one is bored in order that they come to me and quickly amuse me. I am already not talking about the fine, aesthetically developed taste which children have in such a situation and so forth.

All the same, if we return to the theater The Road, they, of course, are still a very noble variant, because in general they began from a theater club where the fellowship of people was valued and everything was wonderful. But what were they compelled to do? They created *The Stone Garden*, based on Japanese poetry. Well, this is a different matter, if we begin to look into the merits of the production. It seems to me that it is itself imperfect as an artistically complete work, but it is, undoubtedly, interesting as an attempt. But what is happening? They cannot perform it. It is nonsense if they perform this production once every six months. I cannot imagine that the actors of the Vakhtangov Theater would have played *Princess Turandot*[34] (beginning in 1921) once every six months. There would not have been such a play then. Why is The Road compelled to perform that way? Because the rent for the location needed to show this production is unusually high. And if, in principle, they perform this production for free, all the earnings go to pay the rent. What is more, it is necessary, most likely, to especially emphasize--the politics for me are in no way understandable. When a State theater and a theater-studio are at the same location, the theater-studio pays far more to rent the space than the State theater.

Stenberg: Whose fault is this?

Markova: As in many other cases, we cannot say who exactly is at fault. There is no such paper with some kind of signature on it. On the other hand, it is understandable. Probably this money does not go into somebody's pocket, or it must be that the cost of the location is really that expensive. But if a State theater is performing there, then the State takes a certain percentage of the rent for itself, and then it is cheaper for the theater itself. That's all.

That's the way we have outlined one extreme. It is that much which preceded the appearance of the theater-studios and before the abnormalities began to complicate this process today. On the other hand, time went by and a new generation grew that also had the natural desire for self-realization. Moreover, it was already completely obvious that the State theater received this generation and its culture at "bayonet points." So when the possibility appeared to open one's own theater, very many theaters were organized by very young people, and for a season they appeared, lived a while, and fell. Very many, and for a lot of various reasons, it seems to me. Several quite quickly shouted their full. They had no personal program, neither aesthetic nor spiritual, none. They simply did not have enough for the long haul. They still, most likely, will search for it. Others essentially did not have enough professional experience, working experience, in order to make a creative undertaking which pays for itself. That is, either they did not want to work or were again sick of having to work on some kinds of problems. They thought that there is none of this in the creative process.

But there was a moment when a sufficiently large part of the creative youth was leaving official life by all possible means, the forms of official life. And if some kind of theater circle was created, then it was not affiliated with the Palace of Culture, where everything is official, where everything is regimented, where it is necessary to present the scripts for approval, perform once a week, where the location is bad and so on and so forth. It is far more comfortable, you'll agree, to gather in a well-furnished apartment, especially if it is large and the hosts are the sufficiently independent parents of the child. And the moment of life, as adapted to the stage, is worked out. "Apartment theaters" are varied, but the moment of theatricality, it seems to me, is always present there. But the usual understanding of theater, the division of the public and the audience, does not apply here. Everyone was both audience and actor. A general performance would take place in which all would take part. This, as the sociologists say, is a small colloquium, which has chosen such a form of existence. Of course, the appearance of such groups to the public can be very explosive in that they very much direct attention to themselves with pretensions toward sensationalism.

Akhmat Rashidovich Bairamkulov and Alla Grigor'evna Minina
October 5, 1989
VOTM

Bairamkulov: I have never spoken about it aloud. I am speaking now and it is difficult for me as I formulate it. I am catching myself on paradoxes, on contradictions, I mean.

When these wonderful processes began in this country, they are truly wonderful; it is now reported in the newspapers. About five years ago, nobody dreamed that the situation in Afghanistan would end, and that it would be possible to talk about it. We could talk about it when we gathered in the kitchen, with friends, or in the theater to hear the word of truth. Why was the theater so popular? Why were people so eager? Why did they read? Through *samizdat*[35] books were published, read, and so forth. It was possible to hear the word of truth, the gospel.

Stenberg: So the influence of the theater was genuine? Even if one word was heard?

Bairamkulov: Yes, of course. When changes in our country began to take place, people began to think about the theater and those who served it; those who work in the theater also began to think, "Why have we had no rights for so long, why, in essence, do we have to live exactly as we lived before, absolutely repeating [everything]?" And today in the theater certain phenomena have become popular which were never in the theater before. A theater collective gathers, votes against the director, he's gone, and they demand another. This is something like a democratic process which seems to be good. The new director, to tell you the truth, is not always better. But there is a contradiction here. Theater art is nevertheless the power of talented people headed by a leader, by a leader with power. Nemirovich-Danchenko put it this way: "The director is the interpreter, teacher, and organizer." And he must be made up of all these. If he is a bad organizer, then he will not hold it all together, and the machine will break down. He then will have to be cruel and step on the heads of others in the name of some kinds of goals.

Stenberg: In the Russian theater there is a tradition of the director being all-powerful. But if VOTM gives money to some kind of organization, is a leader necessary?

Bairamkulov: Of course he is. An organization like VOTM, of course, relies on the concept of a leader, because without him it is simply impossible to establish a studio. The theater, you will agree, is a group headed by a leader. And thus, STD was formed on this wave of change. All theater people joined this union and decided to defend their constitutional right to work--for creativity, for freedom of speech--and to defend the interests of its workers. And on this wave, some financial possibilities appeared at STD, that is, money, et cetera, et cetera. Just then they decided (they came up with some happy invention) in Moscow to establish such an All-Russian Association of Creative Studios [VOTM] in Moscow, in the center. There are affiliations in Leningrad, Petrozavodsk, Voronezh.

This system attempts to counter something in the general theater process. And I ask, what is the general theater process in Leningrad and the studio movement in VOTM? Is it the desire, all the same, to attempt to organize a theater, the very structure, the interrelations, the working out of an artistic program in some other way than it was put together in the traditional governmental system, in the State theaters? That is, one person will appear, then a second, a third, a fourth, and they will stage something--they understand that they are all of one mind. They have shared points of view concerning art, life; something draws them together, and they want something. Earlier, no matter how you would get together, no matter how much you wanted, the result was minimal; it was practically impossible. And now there is the possibility that one does not have to come to a State theater and ask its director, "Please, include me in the plan. I have several ideas." Rather, you go to your friends, colleagues, equals, and say, "I have some ideas, I have some people, actors, I would like to try myself."

Stenberg: There is a great difference?

Bairamkulov: The difference is great; it was impossible to do this in a State theater earlier, and even now one cannot. And further, in order to take this decision, you have to provide the person with the opportunity to either stage the play or not. The mechanics have been devised (and you have read most likely the rules and regulations of VOTM) so that not just one member of the Board--the head director looks at you--"I like you" or "I do not like you." "I will give" or "I won't." No. The Board of Directors gets together headed by Kolia Lavrov. And there, in essence, on the Board of Directors are the respected theater people in Leningrad. There we have the dramatist Liudmila Razumovskaia, Kolia Lavrov, the actress Shuranova, the critic Elena Alekseeva, the actor Sergei Vlasov, the artist

Sasha Orlov, and the famous director from BDT (Bol'shoi dramaticheskii teatr) Boria Mad'ian, and so forth. In essence, there is the attempt to work out on a democratic basis some kind of democratic view demanded when a person arrives. That is, it is already difficult to blame this group of people for petty tyranny, for the "I want it my way." No. It is namely this kind of organization which tries to be objective. Although, you know, that is almost impossible in the arts. Someone is always insulted. Perhaps what is most frightening is that it can happen in the world of art.

But this is the optimal version, it seems to me. This is one of the main tendencies, in general, in the existence of VOTM. And the person, coming here, is not curbed by any kinds of constraints, neither censored nor organizational. This person is free. That is the very same attempt at freedom--in the theatrical world--which is going on right now in the country. And in the regulations [of VOTM] it is written that we will show a preference for those ideas which were neglected earlier in the design stage, interesting forms, not those duplications, as, well, the State theaters, the traditional theater. We have really grown accustomed to realism. Speaking truthfully, I am also a realist, and I think that there is nothing greater. But realism which is not base or vulgar--the realism of Kandinsky, the realism of Picasso.

Stenberg: What about the production in the theater Derevo?

Bairamkulov: I do not accept it; these are searchings which are foreign to me. They have the right to live and let them exist. Perhaps I am a person from another era, another generation. And at the same time we have a very unusual production, *The Dumb Show* by Sergei Dreiden[36] which is closer to me. A forty-five-year-old man does this. The young people there [at Derevo] are super-extra-modern, and they are so far out on the edge that there is nothing beyond them, to use one of our sayings. But you understand, it seems to me, that . . . I will formulate my own thought and want to say it. In Moscow . . . I am afraid to say it, because they may take up arms against me. In that sense the word "charity" earlier was pronounced somehow disdainfully with regard to the theater. The theater is not a charitable organization. "We are professionals. Why should we be engaged in charitable work?" It seems to me that the root, the meaning of this word is to create good, and to pronounce "charity" with scorn, it seems to me, is incorrect. And in this sense, I look back at my own fate and at the fate of my comrades with whom I studied, worked, et cetera. I met dozens of people who were out on the street. And in this country, unemployment was never discussed, and in principle it doesn't exist, but it always was in the theater. I know, I repeat, dozens of actors thrown out on the street without any means to exist, without work. And it is so degrading to beg. And it's not only actors but directors as well. And these are very vulnerable links of the chain in the theater, because a painter, for example, can find work for himself.

Stenberg: In New York it's also very difficult for artists to find work.

Bairamkulov: By the way, I recently saw a television program, maybe it was "View" or "The Fifth Wheel," and the subject was wonderful and instructive. In one of the Scandinavian countries, either in Sweden or in Denmark, they let the unemployed person act in movies. Not because he is a genius, but to let him work. I was startled. And the result is not important. If it is wonderful, then that's very good. And if not, it's not important. The main thing is that the person did work and received money and felt himself to be a member of society and did not have a sense of inferiority, but rather a feeling of self-worth. And in this sense, when actors and directors were roaming in herds and were not able to come somewhere to ask for work, it was terrible. And in this sense, the second action of VOTM is a kind of dialectical connection with the first. You cannot separate it. On the one hand is the dimension of art and on the other hand, the dimension of charity, to create good for its own workers.

The discourse was interrupted by a phone conversation.

Honestly speaking, about four times, probably, I have found myself on the street in Leningrad. Simply at home without any money and living on my wife's salary. And to beg is degrading. And besides, you beg and depend on this theater. I was speaking about this in the beginning. If he [the director] does not like you, he will throw you away and there is nothing you can do, and no kind of union can help you, especially the professional union, which was a fiction in the theater. Do you understand? And it seems to me that in the State theater, the situation is not good. And when STD itself gathers and can help its very own members, why not? After all, any theater is based on three or four or five outstanding people; they determine its face. But they could not exist without the great ballast of middle and average artists or actors. And what if he, the average actor, is the one who must be thrown out on the street? And after all, in essence, that is how it was. A director comes to some theater and brings with him five or six actors and says: "So, remove these, these go there, these go here." And where? Who will think about them if not STD? I want to write about this in detail in order that it not be so cruel and vulgar. I feel that now I am debasing the theme, but I know that such a philosophy of theater . . . this is interconnected. On the one hand, there is the direction in the search for new forms of art and for the full value of the artistic life. That's what I was speaking about, but at the same time the combination of this and charity are interconnected and determine the uniqueness and character of VOTM itself.

Minina: Get back to the structure. The tape will soon run out.

Bairamkulov: The structure is very simple. There is the Board of Directors, which consists of seven members, and we would like more, because very often people are busy and cannot look into things.

Minina: And how much money do they receive?

Bairamkulov: They do not receive any. It's volunteer work. But as Director, I receive money, unlike the other members of the Board of Directors. But I can distribute money, because it's my work, my job.

Stenberg: Is this a volunteer organization?

Bairamkulov: Yes. In principle, this is a volunteer organization. With public money, with money from STD, we bought this building and we paid a lot for it. Namely, with this money we completed the project of reconstruction and now we are reconstructing the building, and two halls will be built here.[37] But you know, Douglas, the situation today is very complicated. There were rumors in Moscow. "What is it that we are wasting money on? Let's not waste money on it but on something else." Because there is such envy, and envy is a feeling that can destroy a lot of beginnings. I'm afraid that . . . Right now, in November, we will defend ourselves in Moscow, and the whole structure will be discussed there. Thus, Douglas, this is what the structure looks like. And further, proposals are appearing, groups are arriving, and we are looking things over. And if we see something beneficial in this, we give them two years [to do something].

Stenberg: Yes, this is the immediate agreement. And how many theaters have you helped?

Bairamkulov: Since we have only existed for a year, we have only three theaters. In the first there are fourteen people, in the other--four, and in the third--two. There are three little theaters. We want to build still another little theater by the summer. But we will not have the possibility to do more, because in two years there will already be other demands and candidates. We will say to these theaters, "We helped you as much as we could and more so." As we say here, "Fly as you wish, only take care of your wings." Then further, we release them to life, let the State help, so let them attempt to have their own repertoire, that they have command of all their plays, to secure in one way or another a roof over their heads, to form themselves if they are artistically sound.

Stenberg: And does this new artistic movement interest people? They say that last year people rarely went to the theater.

Bairamkulov: To the theater in general or to VOTM?

Stenberg: In general.

Bairamkulov: It seems to me, Douglas, that this is continuing right now. Thus, yesterday we canceled a performance. I received a report and we had to do it, because there were only sixteen people in the audience.

Stenberg: And what must be done, do you think?

Bairamkulov: Recently there was an interview on the radio, and now I'll repeat what I said. There are objective processes, because earlier what people could only hear in the theater, now can be read, seen, and observed. Their hands are untied, and they are able to occupy themselves with some material demands. It is best not to go to the theater, but to do something, to work, to earn money.

Minina: Leningrad television has become so interesting that it is impossible to tear oneself away from the television, because there are a lot of political broadcasts and very interesting artistic programs. And they, honestly speaking, are more interesting than the theater today. The theater is not adequate enough to give something to either the mind or to the emotions, as television is doing today. That is the situation in Leningrad. Thus, yesterday there was a program from the United States about the United States, and the commentator said that Leningrad television is known in France, America, and everywhere. "Six Hundred Seconds" is already being quoted in the United States. And what should we say if it is about our life?

Bairamkulov: Yes, this is essential. I recently visited one of my Leningrad bosses on whom our well-being depends. And we still need to secure some rooms. We have problems here with apartments. This boss sat and said the following phrase: "In general, why do we need a theater? Nobody goes to it." This is such a narrow-minded, philistine, and consumer-oriented view of the theater.[38] Let it be, as long as it has something to offer. And when people will stop going to it, we will shut it down. That cannot be. Culture, the theater culture, is not something that depends on attendance, since the theater develops according to the same laws as in nature and society. It has its own repetitions, its own rises and falls.[39]

Consider this image: an apple tree cannot provide apples every month. Just now in September, it has borne fruit, and in October, November, during the whole winter it is necessary to look after the tree. Again, in the fall it will again bear fruit. The theater organism is just the same. Yes, it had its period of ascent and now is the calm. It is necessary for us to look after it, and to support the spirit in it, and it will still be necessary. This boss speaks in vain. Because, you bet, this theater will still be necessary in our life.

All the same, Russia is made up of paradoxes. All the same, it is made up of unforeseen processes. On the one hand, the theater will be necessary. And on the other hand, there is some kind of betrayal of the theater. It seems to me that there must be some kind of fidelity to the theater, and one must be with the theater not only in its ascent when it is going well, but also when it is going poorly, as now. And this is why the people have rushed away. There is no money. One director gave me a list of actors in order that I raise their wages. I want to do this, but I can't. I have already raised them, and I can't anymore. The actor, after having graduated from the theater institute, having received an education, receives one hundred rubles.

Douglas, you most likely already have an understanding of our financial affairs. One hundred rubles is nothing. It is, crudely put, the level of poverty. Officially, it is sixty rubles. But sixty rubles is no longer poverty; it is nothingness. That is what it means to live as a beggar.

Stenberg: And how are they able to live?

Bairamkulov: They live poorly. Very poorly. They live in monstrous conditions. All the more so if there is a family. They are all running after work, some on the radio, others on television. This is in the best case. I know many who work as custodians. This is normal for America. But we have a different psychology. People react to this disdainfully. Once you are sweeping the streets, you are plebeian, a second-class citizen. We still do not have any other psychology. To work as a waiter, to wash dishes, and the next day to work on scholarly activities; in our life, this is still not normal, and people still do not accept it.

Stenberg: A person who loves theater is able to respect this.

Bairamkulov: Yes. Really, only a love for the theater supports them at this insignificant, degrading work. Nevertheless, to come to work, to rehearsal, is to be true to the theater. I have been disappointed with much. Life brings discoveries and disappointments, but one thing has remained throughout my entire life--I love the actor. This is the one profession with which I have not been disappointed. Here the combination of their abandon and their dependence is nevertheless wonderful. That is why, most likely, I agreed to work here. If there were no such love for the actor which rests somewhere in my soul; it's not something which I have thought up in my mind. It is in my heart. I myself acted a little.

Stenberg: So Nina Zarechnaia is a positive character in *The Seagull*?

Minina: "Bear your cross and have faith."

Bairamkulov: Yes, it is so. "Bear your cross and have faith." This is the only way. And when there is no cross, when the actor returns without a cross, when he arrives and when things are good for him, then he ceases to be an artist.[40] God prevent the actor from . . . as soon as he has a sense of well-being and acquires power, and an actor with power is most terrible-- when an artist has power, he is finished as an actor. On the one hand, it is an abandon and an attempt to break away, and on the other hand, once he has found rights and so forth, this leads to narrow-mindedness, to a philistine view of life, to a kind of complacency. And I do not know where the pure truth [istina] is here and where the truth [pravda] is.[41] You were absolutely correct when you mentioned Nina Zarechnaia. Treplev and Nina Zarechnaia are the most normal people in their theater world, although Chekhov does not have such incorrect divisions. But on the other hand, there is Arkadina. She arrives at the performance as the accomplished master, although perhaps she is acting that way, and maybe she is not that way. It's possible to understand either way. She arrives as the center of attention and the suffering of the young man, for whom this performance is life and death, and the worried Nina, for her this . . . So, if you will, who is the artist among them? Nina is in a higher position. But this depends on one's point of view. I can only ascertain the plot, although it is also not so simple.

Minina: I think that we must tell Doug about our structure, about our organization. We have three studios. The studio is one element of our work. In addition to the studios, we have productions which are performed once. The director comes, brings his application, talks about his idea, and if we like it, and as a rule we try not to refuse anyone, we give them the possibility to try it. We provide him with a stage and money in order that they be able to stage their production. We do not provide permanent support. They receive their wages from us and are counted in our ledgers. They do not receive a lot of money for rehearsals. It's about two rubles per rehearsal. Is this so Akhmat?

Bairamkulov: Yes, about two or three rubles.

Minina: This depends on the category of actor, but all the same, the pay is small. And when they are ready, we look at the performance, and if it seems to us that it will work, we provide the means. This is money at the expense of the Creative Studios, that is, VOTM. We organize the run of the show, that is, we provide the opportunity for the public to see the run. We also have a feature, such that, right now we have several shows running while one is in rehearsal. We are also continuing this line. And we still have the opportunity to buy prepared productions. That is, when someone comes and shows us a production which is ready, we are able to accept it and pay for the prepared work.

Stenberg: How many places do you have in Leningrad? You provide the stage and so forth?

Minina: We are trying to do this. Although it is very difficult, we are trying.

Stenberg: Do just a few theaters have their own stage?

Minina: Yes. We have few theaters which have their own stage. The theater-studios, basically, do not have their own stage. They wander where they can.

Bairamkulov: In half a year there will be a more advantageous situation, when we will have our own theater. When we will have our own theater, it will be easier for us. On someone else's stage, the audience has not grown accustomed to you. And so [on our own stage] we raise our own audience. "They beat a path," [to us] as they did to BDT from Nevsky prospekt. A path will be beaten this way as well.

INTERVIEWS

Stenberg: This place will be alive.

Bairamkulov: Douglas, do you know why this will be a lively place, because in the traditional theater where there is one director, he determines the direction and everything that was not even expected is connected with this director. I am not talking about the quality of the performance; this is one person. And if we anticipate ten shows, then perhaps nine of them will be shelved, and one will go up. But these nine will be different and that difference is the main purpose of VOTM. The difference suggests that the directors will also be different, different directions, a different level both professionally and methodologically; the production is based on all of this. The ideas as a whole are based [here, he points to a VOTM poster] . . . Why do we have this, and this, and this, as a group. If they differ, it will be a rainbow. And the difference will be in VOTM. In another theater, it is only this or that. And here one person comes one day and another the next--all the colors of the rainbow.

Stenberg: VOTM supports both traditional and new productions?

Bairamkulov: Yes, we would. And in this is the whole idea of VOTM. Here it is possible for this and that aesthetics to coexist, though they are very different.

Minina: It seems to me very essential that our organization not be commercial. It is not our aim to make money. As distinct from other theater-studios, which insist that they must have the possibility to make money in order to exist. I have already told you that financial self-support in the theater will lead to no good, that's a fact.

Bairamkulov: A theater cannot exist without patrons. Patrons are needed.

Vadim Zhuk
November 9, 1989
The Stanislavsky Actors' Home

Stenberg: Here's the first question: In what way does the theater of today differ from that of the past?

Zhuk: Theater in general as a concept? The theater of Leningrad? How it differs today from yesterday?

Stenberg: Yes, yes.

Zhuk: Years ago in the sixties, when I became a theater spectator, and then in the seventies, when I became experienced as a theater spectator, the theater was some kind of building. It was the head director, actors attached to this theater. There were several definite leaders in the theater life of Leningrad. There was the famous, outstanding BDT and its great head director was Georgii Aleksandrovich Tovstonogov, who provided us with a great number of amazing programs. At that time the concept of "the ensemble" appeared in Leningrad, because he created the ensemble of actors, created the troupe, which was as indissoluble as a chain. By the way, he staged a wonderful American drama, Miller's *The Price*, which was hammered out by one such chain; it's a famous script, do you remember it?

Stenberg: No, I don't.

Zhuk: Well, here was a person, very erudite, with a feeling for direction from birth, a person of colossal culture. And that was the BDT. There was the wonderful Pushkin Theater which also in the sixties . . . it already was very bad, because it was a theater without direction, but in it there were still powerful masters: Cherkasov, Tolubeev, Simonov, Merkur'ev--these were top actors; actors who came as if from the past, from the Romantic theater; actors who had a genuine following. These actors could participate in any performance, and it would be successful.

There was also the theater of Nikolai Akimov, a very caustic, a very sarcastic person of the Teatr komedii.[42] There were not very good actors there, and perhaps great drama was not always staged there, but the humor of Akimov itself and its sense of life--it was also its own theater.

There were the timid beginnings of other directors, which, in general, were not deciding anything in the theater life of the city.

Now everything has changed sharply. Now a new leading theater has appeared. This is the theater of Dodin, as you know, of Lev Dodin, the Malyi dramaticheskii teatr. But here is the paradox: theaters have been permitted to see the world, and the world has been permitted to see our theaters, but we hardly see Dodin's theater. Americans, Japanese, Swedes, and Frenchmen see it more than we, and this is wonderful. But all the same, it seems to me that the theater must exist in its own place; otherwise it will never grow up, especially the Russian theater which is very tied to its roots. Pull it out and it cannot live without its roots. Although, I repeat, it has class, it's a real theater, and Dodin has created an ensemble (and perhaps the BDT which was dying long ago). The death of Tovstonogov only finished the process, because, well, as you of course know very well, a theater always has its life span, and this theater, of course, has already reached its age, after which it is in decline, that is, of course, it's already going down.

As it is, there is no Teatr komedii. There is nothing interesting right now. At the Pushkin Theater there is also nothing interesting. But on the other hand, there has appeared the broad movement of the theater-studios. Here the permission [to function], unfortunately, can decide nothing, because if there is only desire, without talent and a position, it will lead to nothing. Several years, four years ago, when perestroika began, I wrote such a song:

> Yesterday's "cannot" has ended
> Everything now, kids, has become possible
> We have leapt from the slime to royalty
> And conduct ourselves carelessly

And further there were some similar lines and the refrain was:

> Everything is possible which yesterday
> We did not even dare to think about
> The time of fulfillment is coming
> The time to achieve goals

> Something, kids, is just not right
> Where are our boundless ideas?
> Nothing except the little membership card of VTO
> Is our life in the theater

VTO--this is the All-Russian Theater Society--that is, everyone had a great desire: "Yeah! We are allowed. Yeah, now we will burst our shirts wide open and do everything we want." And things have turned out to be without such strength. Perhaps, it is because that, for a long time, we were not allowed, and, one can say, that it was already dying in people. Maybe it's because there is simply more desire in people than ability. But if one takes a look at the studio life, there is nothing interesting. Have you read the eighth issue of the magazine *Teatr*, the article?

Stenberg: Yes, I have it.

Zhuk: The title is a line from my *kapustnik*.[43] Yesterday, you saw the sketch, "'What should we do, Vladimir?' 'I do not know, Konstantin.'" In fact, Vladimir and Konstantin refer to Nemirovich-Danchenko and Stanislavsky. And they do not know what to do, and that is the saddest thing of all when suddenly the inner bankruptcy was discovered.

It has been easier for my theater, The Fourth Wall. First of all, because we ourselves, in our own traditions, have been engaged in this business for a long time. Only earlier there was an opposition; it did not allow us to show our work to a wide audience, because there was a lot of politics in it and so forth. We thought that the greater audience would not understand; we thought that it was only our private business and uninteresting to anyone else. We began to show our work to others and people very quickly were growing used to this language. For the first five to ten minutes they do not laugh, that is to say, they come in cautiously, but then they understand and say, "They are speaking my language!"

I relate to people, let us say, to the public, very well. I am convinced that they understand everything, and it is only necessary to arouse it in them. It is not necessary to show them trash, and if every day we present something worthy, then people will simply become worthy, and from this grows the level of perception, do you understand? I never believed that the public is foolish; in no way is it foolish. How can it be so? They are my brothers and sisters, my friends from school, my children and fathers.

Stenberg: This is perhaps from *The Three Sisters* in that if we try to become educated, we will become a little better tomorrow than we are today?

Zhuk: Yes. I am very glad that you liked our show. We really received a good press; in *Teatr* and in *Theater Life* and in the papers. It is unexpected for our genre, because earlier practically no one wrote about it, simply never. And then it is such a strange genre. Is it really theater? I think that that which is on the stage, right here--the stage and the actor, and there the audience, automatically becomes a theater. Why is the theater only Shakespeare with decorations? The important component for the theater is the actor and audience and stage. That's all!

Stenberg: Yesterday, there was a woman in the audience who asked you about censorship. If it existed, what form did it take? Is there still some kind or is it completely gone today?

Zhuk: I do not know; here I can say practically that in the last two years I have run up against it once, that is, when I officially went to present one of our programs for inspection. And when this woman to whom I brought this began to become bothered about trifles, about the most innocent things, I simply spat and said, "That is your business. We will play it as it is written." And this is already, as things are turning out, possible. The "workers of culture" have responded to this by bottling themselves up, to put it coarsely, and they already understand that they cannot go along with it. The other thing, the idea which I first hit upon last night, is [one's] inner censorship. There are some things which are not worth talking about. Perhaps it is difficult to explain, but some situation must take place which justifies discussion; the moment should allow for talk about such things and not simply because it is "not permitted." As an artist, internally, you must understand what is tasteless. I will not joke in this regard about the relations between Lenin and Krupskaia, roughly speaking. I won't. This is not a subject of art. Many people are attempting to perform only this kind of thing.

Stenberg: It is vulgar.

Zhuk: Yes, do you understand? That is, as if everything were possible and your business. Select from this what you can in accordance with your tastes, with your artistic understanding. I do not know. Censorship exists; it must for showing the naked body and for State secrets. I don't know what. But erotica also exist here. My God, how many films have we seen in which the naked body is wonderful and those in which it is repulsive? It all depends on the artist.

Stenberg: Of course. Perhaps, this is a strange question, but I defended my dissertation on Chekhov's major plays. When Stanislavsky and Nemirovich-Danchenko were in the restaurant last night, it was great. Anton Pavlovich, with his world view and so forth, if he were in the Soviet Union today, at the present time, how would he work and relate to everything?

Zhuk: Understood. The question, of course, is not simple. You, yourself, know that it would be easier for Anton Pavlovich, because of his two professions. He was always able to work as a doctor. This is as it was in recent years, when many talented people (who were not able to express themselves in art because they were not given the opportunity) wrote, as they say in Russia, "for the drawer." Do you know this expression?

Stenberg: Yes, like Bulgakov.

Zhuk: Well, yes. We can say so. And very recently they worked as boilermen, stokers, custodians. I do not think that Chekhov would have taken this path, because publishers would be thirsting for his talent. I am practically convinced that he would be here with his conscience, and now people of conscience are desperately needed. For me, he was a person of colossal conscience. He would be ashamed all the time at everything which is being done. And thus, he would write and, of course, would find the words to express artistic truth to us. All the more so, because if today Chekhov is put on with talent, then everything, truth, everything about life, comes together. Not long ago, before going to see Peter Brook's *The Cherry Orchard*, I reread the play, and my hair simply stood on end from the beauty and strength, because Chekhov is beyond politics in any situation. Why does the entire world stage him, and why did you defend your dissertation on Chekhov? Because, yes, he is about Russia, but also about all people, about all human relations, before all else. Of course, he would not lose himself.

It's interesting, you studied only Chekhov's plays?

Stenberg: Well, I read the prose, but . . .

Zhuk: I have always been interested in Chekhonte's leap from his earliest things. Here is this story of the ascent to prose and plays of genius.

Stenberg: Last evening, of course, there was a kind of comedy, but at the same time there were some serious moments, as far as I understood. What do you think, Chekhov's plays, are they not both comedies and tragedies?

Zhuk: You know that he called them comedies, but for me, of course, the word "drama" is the most exact word in my opinion. Because if you call them tragedies, even the final deaths in several plays, it is, all the same, not a tragedy, because tragedy is the death of a great person, a great ideal.

Stenberg: That's right.

Zhuk: There. And for him the little people perish.

Stenberg: Like us.

Zhuk: Like us. Therefore, it is not a tragedy; it is not Schiller or Shakespeare. It is the most powerful expression of drama, as a concept or understanding. It is, of course, marvelous. Ibsen, perhaps in his best pieces, and Chekhov.

Stenberg: And where will the theaters be in five years?

Zhuk: I desperately hope that people, who now have risen to the first step of the ladder, will find their language. Without this, nothing is possible. I do not have in mind a formal language. In general, I do not relate to formal theater very well. I would love it to be alive and about people. The formal theater, as you have seen, well, it's interesting . . . and this, of course, will be a discovery not in a formal sense, but namely an investigation of the soul. They will find something new to say about people. After all, there has appeared such a writer like Petrushevskaia.[44] Have you read her?

Stenberg: No.

Zhuk: Try. You can find Chekhov's motifs in her writing, by the way. She has found a completely new language, a new slice of life. The other thing is that no one has studied how to stage her. I think that they will. Then, it seems to me, in a certain time some kind of new dramatic leader must arise, although this is not imperative, but a new dramatist, just as it happens in the theater. Here, for example, Brecht was terribly popular in the sixties. And the same applied to Anouilh, who was very popular. Now it is not interesting to stage them at present. Or they do not know how to approach them, because they were both great dramatists (I place Brecht very highly), but a director will be found who will provide the turning point which will shed light on today, and a new theater will appear. But in general, of course, the theater for me is when one can laugh and cry.

Stenberg: Just like last night. Well, I do not want to take up your time any more and simply want to say, "Have a safe trip to America."

Zhuk: If it all works out.

Marina Iur'evna Dmitrievskaia
April 14, 1990
Primorskii raion

Stenberg: Does Leningrad need the theater-studios?

Dmitrievskaia: Of course. Of course Leningrad needs the studios. In general, our theater situation was suffocating because we had no normal, organic process for the birth and death of theaters. Everything was stable here. The building of the Aleksandrinskii Theater has been standing since 1832, but it is still standing even though there is no art there. The stability, of course, was terrible ... Leningrad is a very unfortunate city, because for many years it was a city with one theater--the Bol'shoi dramaticheskii. Tovstonogov was the great director, and in the sixties it was a great theater. Then he wanted to hold on to his students and these positions; everything capable of competition was gradually thrown out of Leningrad. People were leaving. There was a very large emigration to other cities. And there existed such a strange official theater situation. And at the moment when the theater-studios arose in the city, realistically the artistic strengths [people] did not exist which would have been able to lead this new movement. That is, the most talented directors like Ginkas, Ianovskaia, Dvorkin--an entire generation, which at the end of the sixties was able somehow to revive the theater picture, was out of Leningrad, in Moscow, with world famous names and so on and so on. Basically, a lot of people left. That is, the place was trampled down and paved over. And it was understood that the grass would not immediately sprout, that is, organizationally, the moment of the studios' rise coincided with a situation [characteristic] of an artistic hole in Leningrad. And thus, this process began in difficulty and in an unhealthy way. That is, those who went into the studios were not the ones who had some kind of artistic programs, but rather the ones who had the possibility to receive work, though they were not gifted, and not because of their artistic non-conformity with set standards. They somehow physically survived in this city. Besides that, the studio movement suggests the development of some kinds of avant-garde forms, among which, for example ... well, when the avant-garde arose in the beginning of the century, it was understood that it was on the very stable positions of the Moscow Art Theater system, Russian psychological realism, and so forth. And the avant-garde arose as an alternative to the Malyi Theater, which was the king of the nineteenth century.

Now, in the last decade and a half an extremely crumpled theater picture has formed. We do not have any clear directions, some kinds of pure forms or programs. The psychological theater exists in some kinds of degenerate forms. The traditions of the folk theater are lost. And the avant-garde must be an alternative to something and not simply repeat what the Western avant-garde has done before. The logic of our avant-gardists seems strange to me. As if they know the theater of the absurd. We have not had the theater of the absurd, but we'll create it. Not because the moment has organically approached as it did in the West, where the theater was moving and moving and finally it approached the theater of the absurd. And the same for a "happening." So let's have a "happening." We've never had the theater of the absurd.

Stenberg: What is arising on this soil? What is new?

Dmitrievskaia: The Moscow and the Leningrad studios have turned out to be on very different levels. We have very good amateur theaters. It is an absolutely special aesthetic with a different responsibility and rights. I really love our amateur movement, the theater The Crossroads and regional theaters. Sergei Rytov had a very good theater in Gatchina where they put on Petrushevskaia wonderfully. This is a special spirit and another means of existence for actors and so forth. It turned out that the amateurs began to want to become professionals when the official opportunity to organize a studio appeared. It's one thing when the amateur performs once a week, because he wants to. But when they put them in the conditions of financial self-support, they exhausted themselves as overridden horses. These studios, for example the Gatchina studio, exist horribly--they simply earn bread for themselves. In general, it turned out that, organizationally, the studios are in a horrible condition. The Western forms can't be used here, and ours are not worked out. They are hanging around in nightmarish conditions without permanent locations.

Stenberg: What do they need?

Dmitrievskaia: First of all, I think it is necessary to decide the organizational and artistic matters. Organizationally, they need permanent locations, of course. In Leningrad there are a lot of theater locations. A list was published in the journal *Teatr*, which Tresser did, just of the theater locations in the city. It is necessary to evict the District Committees and all these cronies, the military, and so forth. That is one story. But when our studios say that the only thing they don't have are permanent locations and the rest is all wonderful, it seems to me that it is far from so. They have a very large deficit of artistic ideas. People often gather there and they are not very professional, and it's impossible to demand any professionalism from them because they must earn money. But the artistic result is such that you wonder, do they really need these conditions? And you get such a closed circle. But the studios, of course, are needed. And our studios have such a conceit, "We are so poor, unfortunate, and you critics bother us." This is also incorrect, because the situation was created for criticism. And now they are just beginning. Look at their first words, first steps, what are they aiming for? What they are aiming for is not very clear.

Stenberg: Where?

Dmitrievskaia: It seems to me they simply want to be theaters. This is clear. Those who do not have work in stable State theaters--they just want some kind of theater, even a bad one. I think that if work were offered to our studios in the State theaters, they would cast off the studio. I don't think the studio is the idea of their life. It's just the possibility of self-realization, which is impossible in theaters, as well as the possibility of not having to go to the periphery, the boonies. I know that in other Russian cities--I travel a lot--they do not have such a large number of studios in, let's say, Sverdlovsk and Gorky, as has multiplied here. But, let us say, in the conditions of a small city, the most talented actors of the existing State theaters come to a studio in order to creatively realize what the conditions of the State theater do not allow them. And there the artistic results in the periphery often turn out to be better. People go there for creativity. But for us, the studios, I don't know, are a place to work, to receive money.

Stenberg: But if a person considers himself an artist, he has to work somewhere?

Dmitrievskaia: He must, of course he must, if he considers himself thus. The question is, is he really such? Self worth and work are different things. And apropos to that is the fact that their situation is very unclear. Let us say, when the studios began to open last year (my students are such an indication--they are lively kids), they and I rushed around to these very studios. And very soon [the enthusiasm] began to fade. They were bored very quickly; they were not interested. If only it were something new. If only our studios worked on the means of an actor's existence, some kind of form. I have not seen everything, it is true, but what I saw depressed me. What is more, I really do not like pretentious art. And in these studios you often see such pretentiousness with minimal realization. It's natural, because there is not another normal theater mechanism. For example, if the studio has no audience, no success, then it should die. But ours do not.

Stenberg: The studios or a State theater?

Dmitrievskaia: Both must.

Stenberg: Some studios die.

Dmitrievskaia: Not very often. They're very tenacious. Of course, there must be a lot. But one would like them to have a variety of people. But, in general, they are orphans, of course, orphans. On the other hand, let's say there is a child and his parents think that he is a good musician, but he is not. Should his parents develop his ambitions?

Olga Kirsanova and Dmitrii Miropol'skii
February 15, 1990
ul. Lakhtinskaia

Miropol'skii: When there was the decision in Leningrad regarding the creation of theater-studios, that experiment, Lev Rakhlin decided to make his own theater. And everything began from this. Actors were selected without auditions, simply from the street. Someone already knew earlier, someone knew somebody and led [that person] by the hand. That is how sixteen people of different ages were selected. Basically they were graduates of the Leningrad Theater Institute, but there were newcomers as well.

Our place of location was the Malyi zal of the Music Hall, the proprietor of which was the papa of our head director. In order to open the theater, Rakhlin selected Nabokov's play *The Event*. It was the first staging in the USSR, most likely. The calculation was such that this would be our important score (strike). But the production did not work out; direction was absent in it. We basically crashed. At the theater's opening we blundered. Then there was the next premiere, *The Period of Residence Is Over*, based on Varfolomeev's play. This was also a non-event in the city.

Then a group of kids wrote the play *We Play the King!* In the beginning it was conceived as a concert of the authors' songs with some kind of dramatic associations, but then the dramatic connections turned out so well that, all the same, they decided to make it a play. The play worked. At the initial reading it was completely accepted, and we decided to work and present the production. And now it is November, the 10th of November, "Law Enforcement Day," when we first performed the production. Well, right here, at last, what we had waited a long time for took place. Really, an event had taken place in the city. Because the resonance set off throughout the city at once. All at once, people began to arrive, tickets were expensive, some colossal prices, people were asking for extra tickets at the metro, and our three-hundred-seat house held four hundred to five hundred people. And they sat on the steps, on short flights of stairs, on attached stools. In general, it was a success. And we lived on and on with this success, did not grieve, traveled to Moscow, and performed there on the stage of the Iablochkin Central Actors' Home. This was a successful appearance. The public supported us and really liked our production. Then they invited us to Yugoslavia to the BITEF Festival.[45] An international festival, very prestigious. We arrived there and also performed wonderfully. And in Belgrade, in Subbotitsa, the public accepted us wonderfully.

Well, naturally some kinds of plans were made, considering that it seemed we had gotten going, had chosen a definite path, and were beginning to search for something else to do, to search for a play. But since, all the same, the head director of our theater had the leading voice at that time, he chose Jean Anouilh's *Generals in Skirts*. In October we presented this production, and again everything fell through.[46] We understood that this was not our own, that it was necessary to quickly search for some kind of way out, that it was either necessary to write a play again or look for a needed drama. And as drama can be difficult, we decided to write again. Once again, the group of authors sat down at the table, and the result was the play, *If You Skin a Cat, Then It Is the Spitting Image of a Rabbit*.

The first thing we heard in the Head Committee was "This cannot happen! The Soviet spectator does not need this, he must not see this, the play is not needed by anyone, it is anti-art" and so forth. In general, "We forbid [it]!"

Stenberg: Who forbids it?

Miropol'skii: The Main Culture Administration forbade it. We set off for Finland. This was the first Soviet theater which had left on a charitable mission for the West. We appeared to benefit an oncological south-west society in Finland. In Turku and Helsinki we appeared for charity. What we took in went to Amnesty International. This was the first Soviet theater which performed on such a mission. A telex of gratitude was received from London, and they said that they would like to see us and were very much supporting such a step.

And then we returned to Leningrad. Even before the trip to Finland they were talking about some invitations to a festival in Jerusalem, and that we had an invitation to Italy, negotiations were in progress with Spain, that they are waiting for us, want to see us, and are interested in us. And then at the meeting after Finland, the head director of the Theater says to us, that "everything is wonderful, but that nothing will come of it, because I am leaving the Theater, I have no desire to know anything, and nothing interests me anymore." We asked, "And what about our new production?" He said that we are unscrupulous people, that he did not want to be associated with us, that we are very bad, that we had put him in a stupid situation, and that he was not going to work with such people. And he left. The director said, "Ah, so. That means I am also leaving. Either--I do not like several of the actors here--I will drive them out and remain [myself], or you stay and I will leave." But the collective decided to remain a collective, because of *We Play the King*. These are the children of the collective, and they did not want to change anyone. We cared about each other.

So then the director left. Our former assistant director was called to fulfill the responsibilities of the director and to continue working with us. A lot of good things were said. "Kids, let's go!" In spite of this, our former director was going about the Administrative Authority, indicating that the theater was finished. However, we continued to work. We continued to rehearse every day. We continued to bring along our new production *If You Skin a Cat*. We were preparing the premiere. The premiere was supposed to have been on the 30th before New Year's. On the 27th our assistant director, fulfilling the director's responsibilities, informed [us] that he was leaving the Theater. He told us the facts: "As of January 1, I am leaving, and I will not help you with an-y-thing." Yes, and incidentally, he said that as of February 1, our lease of the hall would end. That is, "You hit the street." We started, naturally, to ask questions, "What is this? Go where?" They answered, "That does not interest us." And just then it became clear that our head director was leaving the country. At first there were rumors and then everything was confirmed. He is changing his place of residence.

Stenberg: Like a free person?

Miropol'skii: Yes, like a free person, he has the right. Now he will live in Israel and he can create there.

That means the premiere was forbidden to us. They said, "It cannot be for you, because the play has not been presented for approval and the Main Culture Administration has forbidden it." They said that "you can perform public showings." Fine. The kids appeared on television and Ryzhik saw us. The director, Evgenii Ryzhik, called our artistic leader of the Theater and offered his services in the capacity of director. He came to us and began to rehearse *Cat* with us. At that time the Theater was not only occupied with rehearsals, but with running about through all possible steps and stages in order to finally clear up the situation with *Cat*. We went to Moscow and everywhere in Leningrad they showed us the door. And the last thing that happened was the public showing from January 27-31. The public gave us a very high rating. The Finns were again interested in us. But nevertheless, despite the fact that the city supported [us], the city wrote more than one collective letter, and there were so many calls and arrivals at the higher organizations, and nevertheless on February 1, we were thrown out on the street. Together with all of our property, the artists had nothing left. That's the way it was. Such is the history of our Theater for the year and a half of its existence.

This corresponds to the facts. I existed for a while in this Theater parallel with it, not joining the staff, but at the time working for it as a stage artist, property man, and I fell in love with the Theater, in so far as it is a good theater. Moreover, I already knew several of the actors there. Later on I became closer to the rest. In the course of things there, I found my wife, Olga Germanovna Kirsanova. I like this Theater a lot. The conversations with Rakhlin about introducing me into the staff had been going a long time. At this time, I was on the side, like a spectator, although in general, I knew all the details of the theater kitchen as it were, namely of this Theater. I looked at it like a member of the audience and am grateful for the fact that I have my own view of everything that goes on (as if from the hall and from inside). In this sense, evidently, my opinion differs from that of the actors who see only from the inside, to the extent that they see neither the performances nor any of the rest.

At first, according to my appreciation, a euphoric atmosphere reigned in the Theater. The euphoria was based on the fact that very many of the actors had jumped straight from their school days into a professional theater. This, generally speaking, is quite a rarity for our theater world. Because usually it is necessary to be ordered about for a long time, to rush about in some cases, and the years pass [us] by through all of this. The actors are tied up in the studios, the radio, somewhere in the movies, in order to somehow make themselves known. It is very difficult to land in a theater. As is well known, the studio movement is generally helping people to secure work in their chosen profession.

Because relatively not long ago, still about eight years ago, actors were custodians, boiler-house machinists, worked at physical labor for which they were unqualified, and created in the free time off from work or led discussions about art in the kitchen, in the period of "Kitchen Socialism." The way things turned out, there were several mature actors, people who were already getting on towards forty or fifty. They were at one time acquainted with Rakhlin, the younger Rakhlin, studied together, worked together somewhere, because he had already undertaken attempts to become a director earlier. But he burned successfully for a while on this soil and then showed his complete bankruptcy as a director. And like everyone thought, he had calmed himself. The guy is no fool and had to understand that he had had enough of playing games and that he needed to occupy himself with something inconspicuous. He worked for his dad, was noted on paper as somebody at the Music Hall, and his dad took him around on foreign trips. But for us, it is not the same as for you. It is very prestigious, even right now, though it has become simpler, for the theater-studio which has gone abroad, just as ours did, to be number one. And in general, he was fulfilling some kinds of meager functions of the second sound operator's third helper, that is on the very edge of the control panel there was a toddler who had to move back and forth. That is, it was a sinecure. He did not carry out any kind of responsible functions. And he decided to play here in connection with this wave of the studio movement. And it turned out as in the words of our famous poet, "The little boy went up to his father,"[47] the toddler came to his father and the toddler said, "Daddy, I want a theater." The father sighed and said, "Well, then." And the father just had a small hall in the Music Hall, against which a lot of people had a grudge.

The fact is they dropped an enormous amount of money during long-term construction for this building where the Music Hall is located right now. And when the Friedrich Berlin State Palace came, they became acquainted with it and said that for this amount of money it would be possible to build five Friedrich State Palaces. As far as I recall, fifteen years ago they destroyed this movie house. For fifteen years they have attempted to do something with this building. During this time it would have been possible to complete the construction of half of the city. But this small hall appeared. And it is not so good it seems. It is perhaps good on its own. But it has two makeup rooms in all; moreover one is very small. What is more, the entrance to the stairs along which food and drinks are taken to the buffet is located in that very lobby where the entrances to the makeup rooms are. And besides that there is nothing in the hall except for the coat check. There is no place to sit, no buffet, nothing is there--the men's and women's toilets, that's all. Nothing more, but these are trifles when compared with the fact that most of the theaters in general do not have anything.

The other thing (as luck would have it, because we have already become better acquainted with Rakhlin); the way the troupe was selected cannot be explained through ingenious intuition. The troupe is with a capital T, because a very interesting collective gathered. Several mature actors and an overwhelming majority of young actors between the ages twenty-two and thirty-five. For many of them the theater had not panned out. They had not endured grief and did not know what it is to be unemployed. That is, these are people who, perhaps too early, came to believe in their own genius, thanks to the fact that they were taken straight from their school days to this very theater, and if you will, to this wonderful hall. They did not wander for a while, did not search for themselves, did not search for their place and then fight for it. That is, it is as if they grew up in broth and continued to exist happily in this broth--in a relative broth compared to that which we have for the majority.

And the troupe began to work. The first performance, Nabokov's *The Event* (a certain part of which I wrote personally), but now I am speaking as a member of the audience. The production produced the impression of a complete absence of direction, and indeed that is the way it was. That is, the actors did a number of very interesting things, but as a whole, nothing remained from Nabokov, from his meticulous Russian. Secondly . . . well, a failure or not, it was such an ordinary thing.

And an explosion took place with *King*. I truthfully saw *King* about fifteen times and besides that, well parts, because it is a great pleasure to walk through the Theater, and moreover by pieces in progress, because there were my favorite spots which I would pass by quietly, sit or from behind the curtain watch and revel [in it all]. Eleven people on stage, and it is possible to watch the production due to the number of characters. And then you already begin to relish the separate details. It was never a stiff (frozen) production. What was written in the beginning was completely different from what appeared at the premiere. And what appeared at the premiere is completely different from today. That is, the production lives, is constantly altered. Some kinds of songs, some kinds of pieces are changed, something goes away, something is introduced, some kind of successful find appears, and it is strengthened. That is, this was a wonderful process of a laboratory of action. That is, we constantly followed the production as it presented itself. It was very spontaneous; that is, literally every word was there. If one is to value it objectively, perhaps it smelled a little like an agitational play for those times, although this was not that long ago, and now people are fed up with this. And just then, when there was the blossoming, there was not enough of this sharp material about us, about today, and about things in general, in order that all the questions come to the surface at the same time.

Here, of course, the kids' songs played a very big part. Two completely different performers wrote the songs. Somebody sees in the style of Boria Vishnevskii a parallel with Boris Grebenshchikov, and Maksim Pashkov has something of Aleksandr Bushlachev. These are two popular comrades, one of whom died in '87. He committed suicide by throwing himself out of a window. The fact is that I knew him in '83–'84. Already then he was saying that it was time to go and lie down under a tramline, because it was impossible to live.

Kirsanova: As distinct from those prototypes which we named, they are actors in the best sense with a great professional training. Not only can they sing, they can act as well. This is essential.

Miropol'skii: But without a doubt Maksim Pashkov and Boria had two of the most interesting acting parts in *The Event*. It was simply a light in the little window when compared with what the rest created. . . . Thank God

Nabokov did not see it like this. And then again on the one hand a new phase of eternal euphoria started, because the bitterness of the first failures somehow was quickly forgotten. After *King* the Theater lived practically from *King* to *King*. But *The Event* did not work out, and Rakhlin evidently understood this. *The Event* was performed four times a month. In a general context, twenty-two to twenty-five productions a month is scanty. Especially as there were several actors occupied there who were only performing in this production and nowhere else. They were feeling good about themselves, financially as well, but more about this later. That is, *King* rescued the Theater. And everyone knew it as the Theater named *We Play the King*. Everywhere it was possible not to know what else the Theater was staging, but *We Play the King* (this was the poster of the Theater on which it passed through Yugoslavia very well), and through the efforts of Inna Rogach we landed and performed this production in Finland which we had been afraid to take there.

First of all, the Finns are famous for their peaceful character, and secondly, what are our problems to them? Because this was very keen for us and it was completely unclear as to how they would perceive [it]. And to our surprise they accepted it; there were wonderful reviews in the press. And the constant full houses such that it was physically impossible to copy the advertisement. That is, there is something in it, most likely, some such thing, that touches a person who lives in a completely different world, with completely different worries. Because in this measure they perceived that reality which we showed them on the stage, though this reality is ours. They grasped it as our acting kids do, with [their] humble pay which equals the cost of a pair of women's boots, who arrived in Finland and with open mouths looked at the toilets for invalids, at the things which are most natural for a Finnish person. They looked as if they were idiots, because they could not imagine that meat can be such a color. So much has already been said about this that it does not make sense even to talk about it. But this is what I heard from them, and it is a blessing I did not land there, because at that time I was just affiliated with the Theater and not part of it. They arrived and for a week I heard from Olga that the meat depicted is not just for show, but that is the way it is. This was a shock. And the prices and the level of earnings. And there is nothing surprising in the fact that a person pays attention to this. And soon all is very sad.

And when the boom with regard to *King* began to subside. . . . First of all, something analogous appeared in other theaters, and people got tired of this kind of literature; they wanted something written on current affairs, perhaps, not so direct. And besides, the Theater itself was tired of performing, because this production was exploited mercilessly. And, in the end, as of today, there have been more than 150 performances of *King*.

That is a lot for such a period. It is an awful lot, because the nerves fail which allow such a production to be performed. That is, it goes so far that people leave and talk about the most painful things automatically. This is the murder of the Theater in the embryo. Besides that, there are moments in the text which have already lost their topicality. It is necessary to sit and fundamentally rewrite it, because at some time a queue for soap was talked about, and this theme has since lost its topicality. Now soap is given out for ration cards. There are no such lines for soap--there is nowhere to stand. Take the moment which immediately comes to the surface. And besides, one still wants something; there must be some kind of development.

Rakhlin could become intoxicated by success, but not the troupe. Rakhlin made his name with this production. He is going strong everywhere, Lev Rakhlin. When I made the advertising displays, the kids advised me to make a large separate board, "Make Levy happy, make a big board on which in meter-sized letters will be written--The director of the Theater, LEV RAKHLIN. This way he will look at it and every day will walk by and see this board." By the way, if you would direct your attention to the advertising displays, I shoved in a photograph of *Generals in Skirts*. The Eiffel Tower is there and in the bottom. He was so happy, it was necessary to look beyond his face when he saw it. He placed his money on the necessary number, and the number won. Although with exactly the same sort of success, he could lose. His dad, during a big drunk at the Primorskii restaurant to celebrate the opening of the Theater, led the actors in line off to the side and said, "Well, tell me, what does he need a theater for?" This is the one who has known his son for forty years, thank God. Based on the experience of Lev's previous attempts, he understood splendidly what could come out of this. And he had a notion about this.

Stenberg: Does the situation in Narodnyi dom reflect what is going on in Leningrad with regard to the theater-studios? Is it a complete exception?

Miropol'skii: Here's the situation. I have somehow run over a little with the thought. But it is rare when one can speak into such a nice thing.[48] I am carried away by the process. The Theater can serve as litmus paper for what is going on with the theater-studios. For the time being. The Theater worked in a warm atmosphere. That is, from the very beginning it did not have to struggle for anything. It had everything. Compared with what other theaters had, it simply had royal conditions. Until that time there was a location, there were salaries, which in general are not possible in a theater-studio, because it is essentially a financially self-supporting organization. This means that they finance and compensate themselves.

And the experiment has been conducted formally by the Main Culture Administration since June 10, 1988. Because they bore the child, gave it birth, and then released it into the great life, but without having once corrected it or provided some kind of advice. They received good pay for conducting the experiment but provided no kind of activity in order to assist it. In the well-known sense, they did not love the Theater, did not love it at the same time from all sides.

On the one hand, STD, which wanted perhaps to do something, somehow said, "Kids, perform Chekhov for us and nothing more is needed. If not, it will be bad for you." The wide spine of Daddy Rakhlin did not give us the possibility to say something to them. On the other hand, they again did not love [us] in STD and in general in the other theater-studios. That is mainly because they have such successful people there. And the success in going abroad is shameful. This is also pure human relations.

In a well-known measure, the entourage gloated when suddenly it became clear that the young Rakhlin, having taken the pose of the injured one, was leaving the Theater. The fact is, rumors of his departure had been circulating for a long time, and this was funny. Where should he go? Who is he? To wash windows? He has a big belly which will tip the scales, and he'll fall off the window. There will be nothing for him to do there. Here he has everything. He has his dad, he has a theater in which he can play like a little boy sitting in a sandbox. Why does he need to go there? We refused to have anything to do with these rumors until Rakhlin said, "I am ashamed of you. I do not want to work with this collective anymore. I am leaving you." Well, then it had already become quite clear that he was leaving. Other studios were happy at our misfortune. In January, I became the head director of the Theater. This took place when the director simply said, "I am leaving." And he simply disappeared. That is, the entire administration, all the services of the Theater, except for the creative section were removed from work in general. That is, they simply went out to work one day and then ceased to appear. They did not answer telephone calls, because they were not there. The audience arrived and there were no coat checkers, no cashiers; in general no one. And the Theater found itself in this situation. The actors stood with their mouths open. And it reached the point when everyone--as many of us who were left--we ourselves put up the announcement. We decided in an hour, literally, which play to perform, put up the decorations, hung the advertisement, which I wrote in lightning speed about the fact that such a performance would take place. We ourselves took the tickets from the public, the actors stood in the coat-check; it had reached that point. The studio in a classic guise, the theater of Moli`ere. And in the very same

STD, when I went there to complain about our difficult life, they said to me, "Aha, how pressed you are, you came to us and earlier you were spitting from the top of a tall pine." And suddenly it became clear that in the previous summer, people from STD had repeatedly turned to the director of the Theater and to the head director of the Theater, comrade Rakhlin, when they were organizing the Association of Theater Studios. They turned and said, "Join our association. We are organizing an association, a group of theaters is becoming its founder, we will be doing big things there, and you have such a good theater, you have a name, you have connections, you have everything, let us join together." They said, "We don't need to. Everything with us is good," they said.

We, personally speaking, have been feeling very good since that time, because Rakhlin is going where it is warm, where everyone is happy, where everyone can become a millionaire, if your newspapers do not lie. Lev's buddy now works somewhere in the bookkeeping department of a theater where the director Lev is the first cousin, in my opinion. That is, they have set everyone up and no one has remained insulted. The former head director left for a cooperative and is dealing wonderfully in computers. That is how the situation turned out.

Comrades whom I remember and have known for a long time from the Arts Council turned to me and suggested that I become the head director. I thought about it for two days and then all the same became mixed up in an adventure. Sometimes I have regrets. Exactly a month passed before I officially accepted this appointment. Because everything that goes on in theaters is very difficult. And what happened in our Theater, as I said, is a kind of litmus paper. That is, we ran into the same terrible situation in which the theater-studios find themselves.

Nobody needed anyone while on the one hand the Main Culture Administration demands that all the activity of the theater-studios go through them. And according to the conditions, when they sometimes did direct their attention to something, they had a very tricky device in that the plays which were born in the theater-studio absolutely had to be reviewed in the Main Culture Administration. Although formally they do not have the right to do this. Because the only reason a production may be prohibited or banned is if some kind of constitutional principles are violated in it. There must be no pornography, there must be no calls for the overthrow of the existing regime, there must be no disclosure of State secrets, there must not be any calls for disagreements between nationalities, no calls to war. Here are five reasons why a literary work of art or a work of art in general may be prohibited. If it does not fall under one of these articles, it has the right to exist, and only the audience is entitled to decide whether or not it should go to a production. If suddenly some suspicion arises at the Main Culture Administration that some kind of State secret is being disclosed there, it is necessary to find out from the beginning in order to divulge [it] later. If they have some kind of suspicion there exists a single organization--the Main Administration for the Protection of State Secrets. This means that they then give them the material, they look and see, "Aha, the way the ship Snowstorm is made is written here. This production cannot be shown on the stage." This is how it is ideally. In fact, some civil servant of culture sits in his armchair with a salary of 580 rubles a month while the actress Kirsanova, as a pretty good actress would, for one's information, makes 150 rubles. The difference is phenomenal, almost four times. They sit and receive the unkempt and unusual and at once greet this with bayonets. Why? Because, first of all, a stereotype is most likely at work here, if some such thing gets one's attention, something unusual, it is best to forbid it at once, and all is calm. They say that this will not be. And nobody is troubled as to whether or not they have the legal right. Already this does not bother anyone. They say no and sleep peacefully. They have washed their hands. Because there exists a little proviso that we are obligated to pass our play through them. And such a thing exists.

When it was decided that we would perform a public viewing, what was the difference? This in principle is the very same premiere, only it was forbidden to charge money. We were told, "You can perform, but for free." A premiere implies the sale of tickets and all the rest. "If you sell tickets, we will . . . you, in general, prepare yourself." They made scary faces, gnawed their teeth, and when we performed two public viewings (it was then announced that I had had a small interview in the newspaper *Smena*, in which I had meekly talked about the fact that there would be two public viewings and then two premiere performances) they simply spat. On the morning of the premiere performance, tickets were already sold. At first, by some kind of means, it's not understandable why, in the central ticket booths they had stamped the tickets differently. The name of the play was different; they stamped *We Play the King*. Although even in December it had been announced that for January, during these days would be *If You Skin a Cat, Then It Is the Spitting Image of a Rabbit*. It is unclear why they did this, to serve whom? On the morning of the premiere in the Music Hall they called us from the Main Culture Administration and said, "What's this you have reared for yourselves on the small stage? What are you up to? At your place they are illegally performing shows which are not allowed and they are taking money. This smells like you will be called to account as a criminal. Do you know what will happen to you? Cease immediately!" Here's a question, what kind of relations does the Main Culture Administration have with the Music Hall? Does this include mutual relations with us? And a second question. What kind of relations does the Music Hall have with us? We are renting the Hall from them and are paying them 214 rubles a day.

Stenberg: A day?

Miropol'skii: A day. That is, we were paying up until February 1.

K. N. Chernozemov
February 20, 1990
STD

Stenberg: Describe how you understand this movement.

Chernozemov: It is a very good movement because the initiative is born of some kinds of new theater groups. They have very independent motives of conduct, using the authority of their audience. In principle, there is only one wish which we are more or less realizing. This is the question of quality. Because one of the most frightening problems which has arisen is the loss of theater civilization as such. Because [people] have lost an interest in modern literature, lost an interest in classical literature, and have lost an interest in the integrity of their own literature. And thus this problem is a long-drawn-out problem, demanding enormous energy from young people, namely in the direction of quality, poignancy, and so forth. Because this is work, and it is difficult to work, especially in such circumstances. Because everyone in any event is spoiled by some kind of period in the initial, as they say, love for the theater. But the work in the studio, even if we compare it with the experience of our generation, has always been selfless work--be it the Sovremennik, the Taganka, or the experiments of Anatolii Vasil'ev. This is a surprisingly complicated matter. But in order to move beyond that stage in which the theater market, having arisen, becomes ossified, it is necessary to leave it. This is the prime responsibility of the young people. Such are the conditions.

Stenberg: How do the theater-studios today differ?

Chernozemov: You understand, they differ, above all else, in the interest in drama. Let us take such a group as By a Single Author... it is working on the dramatist Zlotnikov. This dramatist, who is very interesting, very creative, has a mass of all possible qualities. Thus, this group is held together by the fact that it is experimental and is discovering new literature. Let us take the Theater of Real Art, which is connected with an interest in literature. Take *Maskarad*,[49] which has been kept down since 1946. In Leningrad, it simply did not appear on the dramatic stage. And now it has returned. But it is necessary to have character in order to go to this *Maskarad*. Because the troupe is to quite a degree delicate, and there are very serious dangers. Although Goroshevskii is an energetic person and fresh in his thinking and, in general, in his perspective.

As far as the studios that are arising in such completely cruel conditions, in all kinds of basements, they are before all else, interesting due to the fact that they are endlessly energetic. Let us take Tomoshevskii's group [The Comedian's Refuge], which is constantly working on comic material. It is turning upside-down all the obstructions which were related to the real eccentric Russian literature, to old [literature]. We have a very poetic moment and a very gifted person, Tomoshevskii. He has natural talents and everything is therefore interesting.

Let us take the theater The Road on Bakunin 2. There is also a very pleasant reaction, because they perform Albee and they are still small-scale, young actors, that is to say in their own way, completely young. In them there is seriousness, there is a very strong human individuality and this is a very nice thing. But they are still very energetic in the field of experimentation with various forms. Let's assume they have a production in the genre of pantomime, of the dumb theater, a Japanese theme, a lyrical production. Everything here is technically very delicate, thus everything is *kasha* cooked for the first time, although there is a very energetic organizer there who actively works at some kinds of joint-European cultural centers in Denmark, I think. They have started and are developing contacts and right now are about to set off on tour. There is a very good tone there. Moreover, this director, who rose as a graduate of the Institute of Culture, a curious path to a sufficient degree, because he was applying to the Theater Institute, but the level of our entrance exams (it's mysterious); he had to master his profession without theater institutes.[50] He is an artist and has a mass of various merits.

Stenberg: Where do you think the studio movement is going?

Chernozemov: Where is it going? It is going towards the accumulation of theater culture and the sufficiently active avant-garde, because on this side and that it is answering the spiritual needs of the younger generation. They are searching for distinct forms. This is useful because the theater must, to a sufficient degree, be unexpected in its philosophy, aesthetics, and in the craft of the actor. Thus it depends on energy, and for that we have the experience of Ganelin and Bogdanov. This suits me, because we have performances in two directions, in order that the contemporary language be playful and the literature be relevant with the definite and very complicated material associated with contemporary problems.

Maksim Maksimov
March 14, 1990
Smena

Stenberg: How does the studio movement reflect the culture of Leningrad, how does it differ?

Maksimov: I would say that today the movement in Leningrad reflects, in general, not only the cultural life (and not even the cultural life so much as the political and social life). That is, among the majority of the numerous theater-studios in Leningrad, and there are already more than 160 according to the latest data, including all of the most varied small [ones] at the DK, ZHEKs, and REU.[51] Among these theaters there are really, we will say, genuinely ten creative collectives at most. All the rest are not really theaters in the primordial sense of the word, as a kind of. . .

Stenberg: Rock groups, show. . .

Maksimov: This is already a different sphere somewhat. This is also a very significant moment, when under the pretext of a "theater," commercial enterprises for hire are simply functioning while calling themselves theaters; exactly as, let us say, the theater-studio Benefis, run by M. Boiarskii, the rock theater-studio Sekret. But the discussion is not about this. I somehow do not even pay attention to such theaters. This is out of the sphere of our research.

There are very few such theater collectives among those which call themselves theaters, that is, those that put on performances. Basically, there are certain kinds of socio-cultural phenomena, that somehow are absorbing all that is going on, all the aurae, accumulating everything into themselves, and the result of their activity can be the most diverse.

There is the Interior Theater in Leningrad, which is directed by Nikolai Beliak. This is a State theater on an experimental basis. Nikolai Beliak is a very famous director. About ten years ago, he staged several significant productions (*Faust* and *The Little Tragedies*); a number of very classical and cultural productions. During those three years, when this theater existed on an experimental basis, not one production was put on. That is this State theater, the State Interior Theater, did not perform once. One asks, what were they doing? Nobody knows this. There was a time when they staged a meeting (a demonstration) to defend Del'vig's[52] home on Vladimirskii prospekt, which was to be removed. The protest meeting was informally organized and Nikolai Beliak directed it somehow, that is he used his education as a director, his profession, towards the goal of directing this meeting.

There were still two or three detailed events which I do not remember now. The very last is connected with the name of the Interior Theater. During the pre-election campaign they nominated about one hundred candidates for deputy positions. Eighty for local districts and eighteen for the Russian Republic. Naturally, after they came out with such a list, all moreover from the democratic forces, the Culture Administration began to look into exactly what kind of theater this is and why it has existed up to now, and in general threatened to shut them down. I want to say that a kind of theater exists in which there are actors, professional actors, as well as a composer, Aleksandr Zalivalov, who heads the music section. And nevertheless, not one production has been put on. What is more, there is an excellent article about them in the French press. When a group of French film and theater people from the association Fabriks came here, they even concluded an agreement with Beliak about the organization of a joint action, a street action during the spring holiday in the city. They had not seen any of the performances, but the article appeared in the French press. That is this theater is half-mythical. This theater is a legend.

That is one type. Another type is the theater-salon Sankt-Peterburg, under the direction of Evgenii Lukoshkov. I know Zhenia Lukoshkov. He is both a wonderful actor and businessman. Two plays continually run in their repertoire. And now another. This is Lermontov's *Two Brothers*. One can argue as to whether it is a good or bad production, but in essence of course, the goals which they have set for themselves do not concern the creation of productions. The task is completely different--to recreate the atmosphere of the Petersburg salon at the beginning of the century. And for the most part, their repertoire consists of such literary evenings, literary musical evenings. Zhenia Lukoshkov himself is a good reader. He reads Severianin, Kharms, the poetry of the Silver Age. But at the same time, the theaters, which set for themselves the primordial task of not creating some kind of program, but namely to recreate an atmosphere, are not essentially occupied with their destiny. The theater The Comedian's Refuge, of which I am the head of the literary section, is pursuing a similar program to that of Sankt-Peterburg. But, on the other hand, this essentially was not a theater. It was an artist's basement, especially as, they had no pretense for more, although in the course of the last month two productions of value have come out: *No One is Writing the Colonel* by Marquéz and Vvedenskii's *The Ivanov's Christmas Tree*.

There are also even more interesting versions. There is the Theater of Unsolved Problems. Have you heard of it? A certain Vadim Poliakov directs it. It is difficult to say what it is. I have seen only one production of this theater; it's called *Methods of Destruction*. It was absolutely unprofessional, half-amateur, hack-work, action of a low level, basically, based only on some kinds of sharp political moments. And the political verses there are completely ungrammatical. That is, the direction is absolutely zero and there is nothing to say about the acting. This is simply a group of amateurs that is trying to express its relationship to the world. The basic theme is war with bureaucracy. That is abstractly, one sees an enemy in every bureaucracy. This theater is located in a half-ruined building on Ligovskii prospekt. The building, which is planned for removal, has architectural value. But they cannot tear it down only because they have illegally taken it over, occupied it, and stage their performances there from time to time. Besides this, they organized poets' tournaments. There is the goal to create a park of culture, and Vadim Poliakov is one of the members of the People's Front, of the Democratic Union, and many other social organizations. We will say then that this is some kind of strange, unintelligible formation.

I have presented only extreme examples. But if we take even those theaters, which are close to the theater in a true understanding, we have the creative collectives. It is possible here to discover the same tendency. The theater-studio Derevo, under the direction of Anton Adasinskii . . . it is an excellent collective, wonderful. I am always carried away by them when I see, perhaps, the most professional of all the theater-studios. Well, what they do may be called varied. I would call it (I have thus determined it for myself) an attempt on the one hand to recreate the supple images of the present social mythology, and on the other, an original recruitment of the audience. Even that very ritual with the preparation of the plastic mask, this is something different, like a recruitment, the formation of a fellowship, in some degree, conciliarism. Is this a goal of the theater? I do not know. It is very possible that such an image needs to be realized today.

There is a very interesting creative collective theater, Gun-go. Earlier it was called Direktiva. The managing director is Sergei Kormin. This is a street theater, an event-theater. I would define it as an event-theater. They set up happenings in lines for wine. In their own time according to the law of sobriety they carried the situation of queuing to the absurd. They have performed in kindergartens, in a madhouse, in the Bekhterev Institute, also as a kind of psycho-drama. That is, it is not entirely true that this is a theater demanded by a particular social class. They rarely work to order. Perhaps the theater is an event, the most exact definition. They conducted a very interesting event in a park under the title "Reincarnation," in the spirit of cruelty, but at the same time with a candid mockery.

Stenberg: So the movement is quite many-colored?

Maksimov: Very much so. Therefore, I would answer the question as to what degree the theater-studios reflect the cultural life of today in such a way, that they are refracting one kind of a facet, not only cultural, but in general, of the entire diverse social reality.

Vadim Gushchin
December 2, 1989
ul. Skorokhodovaia

Stenberg: Vadim, could you talk about your work and about the theater movement?

Gushchin: Well, to the extent that I was chosen to serve in a public theater organization and work with the theater youth of Leningrad, then naturally I have run up against the problem of the theater-studios. Of course, now, in the last two to three years, this movement has really profited, in as much as the Government has allowed the theaters to come into being independent of State institutions. And naturally, there are a lot of actors who were not able to realize themselves in the State theaters; they did not have work there and were not able to establish themselves. Of course, they all gathered in these theater-studios. It seems to me that this is very good, because the possibility has arisen to begin some kinds of genuinely authentic works of theater art as if in a competing system. Because they are independent from the State and do not receive subsidies and money from it. And in such a way they are compelled to work as the way things are.

A lot of theaters have arisen just now. But unfortunately, in my view, out of this number of theaters which now exist, there are still very few theater-studios which deserve close scrutiny and a high level of appreciation.

Stenberg: Why?

Gushchin: Well, first, there is the main condition in which they came into being; people came who were simply out of work, and they wanted to occupy themselves with something and receive money for it. And thus the studios were not always created according to the principles of the studio. That is, as I understand it, a studio is a group of people who understands some kinds of problems in the same way, they identically feel them, [and] have some kind of leader who takes upon himself the right to stage a production if they have faith in his staging. And it is on the basis of some kinds of general conceptions of life that they work out their principles and their views on life.[53] But now, unfortunately, the majority of theater-studios have arisen according to the principle of unemployed actors. And this is the most important thing.

But despite all this, the theater of Adasinskii, it seems to me, is exactly the kind of theater we are talking about. He professes definite views on life, and in principle, the actors all relate to life, good and evil, in the same way, understand identically their place in life, and search for certain forms to the extent that they think that the theater which now exists has already become sufficiently obsolete in terms of form. It is possible to agree with them, it is possible to argue, but this is something new, it seems to me, which has the right to exist. I, for example, do not really accept it very much, to the extent that I am an actor of the Russian school, we can say.

We have interesting puppet theater-studios, several of them. It seems to me that The House on Trinity Meadow is interesting. There is a series of productions which are not at all considered theater-studios at VOTM. This is an organization we have which provides actors and directors, who, in general, are not a part of any theater-studios, with the opportunity to express themselves. And it seems to me that at the present time a kind of basis for the theater-studios is arising. And right now there are talented people here who have put out several talented productions.

I think that a problem of the theater-studios is that they don't have enough money--too few possibilities for the creation of expensive productions. Although this is also dictated by peculiar conditions, and they create theater, if you will, on a small scale. But perhaps this, too, is good. People are competing.

Stenberg: Vadim, is theater training necessary today or unnecessary?

Gushchin: Of course, I think it is necessary, because an actor's training in the Soviet Union, if good instructors are teaching (we had a good teacher for example), offers not just a genuine existence on the stage. Because, such a genuine existence on the stage is possible for an actor without education if he has talent. There are very many actors in both the theater-studios and amateur theaters. But a counter question: is it possible to write plays without an education?

Stenberg: Shakespeare did.

Gushchin: He had an actor's training and therefore thoroughly knew the entire school of acting. For example, this again is my opinion, it is impossible to perform Shakespeare and, we shall say, Lope de Vega or Moli`ere the same way, because each play differs for a reason: comedy, tragedy, drama. The play demands its own existence. When an actor goes on-stage, he must create some kind of person. Here I, Vadim Gushchin, go on-stage and perform the same way everywhere, that is in *Hamlet*, *Fuente Ovejuna*, and in *The Misanthrope*. I am playing Vadim Gushchin like myself. Nobody is interested in this, because I think that an actor must create definite characters. And even in America there are better, universally recognized roles. For example, Dustin Hoffman (who acted in the popular film *Tootsie*) did not exist as himself. He created the image of a definite person.

It seems to me that an actor with an education, all the more so if he is talented, does not have to rely solely on an academic approach. And even without an education, if he has genius, he can reach that high level of professionalism and spiritual condition on the stage and in film. But the actor with an education and talent knows (and must know in any case when working with good teachers) what distinguishes comedy from tragedy and how to approach a role, what kinds of movements are to be used concretely in this or that role. And there is still another plus regarding the advantage of having an actor's training, apart from anything else, a definite means is created, in which there is the possibility, first of all, to understand yourself, the theater as it really is, and to formulate a definite approach to the theater and to that which the theater must be. In principle, to receive a really genuine education in the humanities and to know theater history and the history of literature can be terrifically helpful, of course. That is, the people who finish the Theater Institute, for example, are greatly different from those who applied. They are completely different people. But the actor without an education, in principle, rarely achieves the great heights as an actor. For example, in the Soviet Union there are not that many cases when actors could somehow . . .

Stenberg: But there are kids today in the theater-studios who do not have a theater education.

Gushchin: Yes, yes. Well, I for example, also worked in the theater at the University before studying at the Institute. I was studying then at the University. What appeals to you? A terrific interest in work, a lack of interest in material things, and fervor. But, you understand, this is what distinguishes a professional actor from a non-professional. For example, the professional actor must perform in two or three productions every day. And he must act at full strength. So when such a theater was formed like the Molodezhnyi, in which there were non-professional actors, they all gradually left, because they could not take that kind of expenditure of energy. You understand? Because every artist going on-stage spends a lot of his inner energy. And they could not stand it and left because the quality gradually fell. Because they were not acting two or three times a week, not even three times a week, but every day, sometimes two or three shows.

And the non-professional actor does not have the kinds of developed resources as the professional, who, if he is lacking something on the inside, is able to achieve it technically. Understand? And the difference lies in the fact that he knows how to achieve it technically. Thus, the amateur productions, for example, are very dissimilar in terms of their quality. Today an actor arrives upset, and it is quite possible that the production will not go well. But the other thing, right now in Leningrad, for my part, is that our professional actors, the majority of them, have a very low professional preparation. But this is something else. The genuine professional actor is not typical of the type who exists in the majority of State theaters. That is my position.

Isaak Romanovich Shtokband
September 19, 1989
Theater Bouffe

Stenberg: First of all, I am interested in knowing how your theater differs from others.

Shtokband: We have a variety theater, a cabaret made up of graduates of the Leningrad Theater Institute. In general, we have a good tradition, the tradition of the twenties, when there were theaters which were founded by artists of the Moscow Art Theater and Stanislavsky, and in the thirties they were all destroyed. Stalin did not like them.

Stenberg: Meierkhol'd?

Shtokband: Yes. Yes. Stalin did not like them. They did not suit his views. That is, during Stalin's time, they ceased to exist. That kind of theater, beginning in the thirties and into the forties and fifties, in general did not exist. There were some kinds of groups of artists on tour, let's say, such prominent artists of the Soviet variety theater as Raikin. Until last year, it had its own building, its own complex, and before it was a touring collective which travels and so forth. But the Theater Bouffe is the first permanent variety theater which we have, at present, in the country which has its own main stage and smaller performing stage, and permanent troupe, and has its own repertoire with more than one production. There are different performances which are presented in their own spaces, which are distinguished from those in other theaters in that these are lesser forms of theater or scene work. These are variety miniatures, songs, dance, parody, jokes, and irony. This is on a small scale, and every production is an independent number. And from those individual pieces the show itself is created.

Stenberg: Do you think this is more difficult?

Shtokband: Yes, it is more difficult. To create a number is more complicated than putting on a performance from a play.

Stenberg: Why?

Shtokband: Because, a number is created from the material of the actor's innate abilities, from what is inside the actor. The number is not composed by anyone. The number is composed by the actor himself. The actor bears its idea inside of himself and creates on his own. Just as the traditional theater begins with drama and is followed by stagecraft, it depends on the creations of Shakespeare, Moli`ere, and Hugo, the actors of the variety theater depend on themselves. He creates from himself. He can invite a composer, a dramatist, and he will say to the dramatist, "You write me such and such a thing," and the dramatist writes what the actor wants, and he tries to reveal to the actor what the actor himself sees in the piece.

Stenberg: Does this depend on the education of the actor as well as his talent?

Shtokband: Yes, talent and education. But I would say that, in the traditional theater, the actor is defended on all sides. That is, around him a big apparatus is at work of dramatists, directors, and set designers, who make decorations, music, and many many other things which serve only the actor. The actor is within the dramatic art; he serves one function, one role. One actor plays Hamlet, the other the gravedigger, the third plays some kind of role with two exits and then does not appear again. He lives in those dimensions or conditions set for him by the dramatist. And therefore his professionalism and mastery are all he needs. He has mastered the actor's profession, and he is able to perform the role which the dramatist or author has written and the conceptions on which he and the director work. The artist of the variety show works in different conditions. He is his own theater.[54]

Stenberg: He must know and understand more?

Shtokband: He must know and understand more. And he has a greater responsibility. He cannot hide behind anyone or any role. He has entered and holds the audience, and the audience either accepts him or does not. An actor in a conventional theater can hide behind the production, director, or author. He serves a kind of function. But for the actor of the variety show there is always a duel between the actor and the audience. He enters the stage as in a duel; he is alone, he holds the audience, and the audience specifically applauds him for his individual creativity. There is always a more direct contact between the actor and the audience. In the variety genre, the actor is the audience's partner. In the dramatic theater, the actor is the partner of another actor. He talks with him, lives with him, kills, and loves him. He is with him. And the audience is somewhat off to the side. And this is easier. It's a little false, a little fake. Perhaps I am not acting very well, but all the same, my partner cannot say that he does not believe me. He says those words which are written for him. But when contact is made with the audience, when the partner is the audience, it is impossible to be insincere.[55]

Stenberg: How can an actor prepare for this if he does not know who his audience will be?

Shtokband: Each time it all begins at the beginning. But that which exists in the theater does not exist here. In the theater the production either meets with success or is doomed to failure. In the traditional theater everything is done and foreseen, while the audience only observes, and here the audience not only observes but lives with the actor, and therefore the actor does not know how his audience-partner will behave. From his first entrance the struggle begins, the struggle to conquer his partner, to conquer the audience. This is very difficult.

Stenberg: Like life.

Shtokband: Like life.

Stenberg: It's possible that an experienced actor . . .

Shtokband: I would put it this way: the experienced actor wastes less strength; the actor who has less experience has not mastered the technique; he must waste more emotion and energy in order to conquer the audience.

Elena Shalamova: They begin to perform in the second year of their training and therefore have the experience in making contact with the audience. Your theater is quite original. The Theater Bouffe, is it joining the movement of the non-traditional theaters, the theater-studios?

Shtokband: No. We are not part of the movement and I will tell you why. If there are so many theater-studios, growing like mushrooms after a rain, so many in Leningrad--I don't know, an enormous number, I would put it this way: they are completing their mission or search, in the field, all the same, of traditional drama, roughly, the dramatic play, which for these theaters is the basic genre. What we are depends on the actor, the drama for us is secondary. That is our distinction. We write the drama ourselves, we compose all of the words which we speak, everything which is spoken on the stage is written by us.

Elena Shalamova: You think that the theater-studios are working towards the return of "forgotten" drama, that is, most theaters are concerned with form, while you are more concerned with the actor. And you are returning to the forgotten traditions?

Stenberg: This theater follows what tradition?

Shtokband: It is the tradition of the crude folk theater.

Stenberg: The *skomorokhi*?[56]

Shtokband: Yes, the *skomorokhi*. If you are familiar with Peter Brook's book *The Empty Space*, he divides the theater into the spiritual theater and the base.

Stenberg: Tragedy and comedy?

Shtokband: Yes. The base theater is the vulgar theater from *commedia dell'arte*. That is one direction. And of course "bouffe" derives its name from buffoonery.[57]

Elena Shalamova: When you were creating your theater, did you have in mind analogies with theater from the turn of the century?

Shtokband: Yes, of course. I will tell you. The first Russian variety theater was opened in 1864.[58] That is, 120 years ago, in St. Petersburg on Nevsky prospekt, where the Palace of Pioneers is now located. In this garden stood the first Russian variety theater. Russian artists came there as well as Italians, Frenchmen, and touring troupes. The tsar allowed all genres to perform except for one. He did not allow the spoken word on the stage. He was afraid of words. He understood that in this theater, it was impossible to follow what the actors said. And in order not to undermine the foundations of the Government, he forbade any words spoken in the Bouffe. "Let them dance, let them sing, but do not let them speak." The tradition of the Russian variety show began with the Bouffe. Therefore, that is the name we have chosen.

Stenberg: Do you think that at the present time, it is better or easier than before to present the forms you wish?

Shtokband: Today or earlier?

Stenberg: Yes. During perestroika or . . .

Shtokband: Yes, right now, of course, there are more possibilities, because practically all censorship has been abolished. It does not exist. Therefore it is easier for us, because earlier all that we did, all that we conceived, had to be written and sent to various organizations, where it was read over and over again. Then they came, watched, and said that everything will not do. But now everything is easier.

Stenberg: How does the education in the theater-studios differ from the instruction in the past?

Shtokband: We have an entire system of theater education. We have drama schools of higher education. I teach in the Leningrad Theater Institute. I am dean and I have my own course, and I educate, and invite you tomorrow to see my students at 8:00. But let's continue during the intermission.

During the intermission of the variety show performance:

Shtokband: This theater was founded in 1983. Before that I worked in Petrozavodsk, in the Russian Dramatic Theater.

Stenberg: How will the theater-studios differ in five years?

Shtokband: It seems to me that today the traditional theater in the Soviet Union is dying. It has done all that it could. And in its place is coming a newer, more energetic, more mobile (not the big, imposing, or spacious), theater-studio. They are experimenting, searching. They have their own brave stride. It seems to me that the future bodes well for the theater-studios. We have theater-studios which began right after the Revolution. Immediately after the first years of Soviet power, a great number of theater-studios were organized.

Stenberg: Where?

Shtokband: In Moscow, Leningrad, among which in Moscow, there were the MKHAT studios. There were the Vakhtangov theater-studios, about which you have certainly read. And then in the thirties they were all destroyed. That is, our Stalin did not love any kinds of experimentation or creative searching. Stalin loved regulations.

Stenberg: Socialist Realism?

Shtokband: Yes, only Socialist Realism, and therefore all searches for new forms were eliminated. They were physically wiped out. That is how Meierkhol'd perished. Now, the time has come when the theater-studios have come to life, small collectives which are headed by a leader, which have their own ideas and thoughts. And thanks to these ideas and thoughts, a theater aesthetics is forming around them. And it seems to me that this is a productive path for us. Because of all the theaters which we have now, the classical theater has become conservative. It is difficult to search for new forms and movements in it. Acting troupes sit there who have worked at the same place for many years. They have grown old, and they are not prepared to search for new forms.

Stenberg: Our actors must independently search for work and do not have the family feeling that the ensemble troupe can provide.

Shtokband: What is good in our theater system? We have permanent acting troupes, the collective. These are people who have worked with each other for years. And it is an organization which is capable of collective creativity. This is good. But theater is a living art. And theater becomes old with the troupe and dies with the people.

Stenberg: As the cherry orchard?

Shtokband: Yes, as the cherry orchard. And the moment comes when the theater which was very good becomes old, and old, and old, no new people join the troupe. And in the end we see that the art of this theater has become tired. Only strong talents can overcome their age. We do not know and do not want to know how old Hemingway is? He is always young.

Stenberg: If relations between theaters of the West and the Soviet Union continue to grow, what kind of influence will it have on the theater-studios here?

Shtokband: I can say that it's a mutual influence, the theater of the West takes something from us and we take something from them. Our directors travel to the West to stage their productions. We tour there. We take something from the Western theater.

Stenberg: In what way?

Shtokband: I will tell you in this way, that the Western theater is more avant-garde than the classical Russian theater. I am not talking about the American Broadway musicals. Basically, if the Russian theater is distinguished by its psychological school, the Western theater is more often dominated by form; the form is more important than the content. We are delighted with form and attempt to borrow that, although it is mutual. It seems that the advantage of the Russian theater tradition is its psychological depth. And often we do not have enough form, as in the dramatic theater, as in the ballet.

Stenberg: The good actor must know his culture and literature?

Shtokband: I do not know the system of theater education very well in the United States of America. But our theater training is indeed higher education. That is, in theater institutes, where except for the mastery of acting and acting technique, there is an entire curriculum of humanities subjects: the history of theater, cultural history, the history of world theater, and the history of world culture. Educated specialists, intellectuals, graduate from the theater institutes. This is our positive feature.

Stenberg: If an actor plays Hamlet, for example?

Shtokband: First of all, it is important to understand philosophy; then the history and the spirit of Shakespeare and the aesthetics of his theater.

---

[1] In his letter of March 4, 1993, Mr. Gushchin writes the following translated from Russian: "It is impossible to live on an actor's salary. A great many actors are leaving the theater and changing their profession. The theaters are in a very bad state. The State provides little financing. Many theaters function through the support of sponsors. But the sponsors also do not give a lot of money. Thus the small theaters either wear themselves out or hardly perform since there isn't even enough money to rent the hall. The actors whom I know are depressed since they don't know what will happen to them in the future. A lot are emigrating."

[2] These Russian artists and scholars gave of themselves to Colorado. For example, Iurii Zaitsev spoke at the Aragon Middle School and lectured on theater and art at Colorado College. Marina Smyslova has met with the Colorado Springs Civitan Club, has spoken at Air Academy High School and Eagleview Middle School, and has served as Head Resident of the Russian House at Colorado College since 1991. Vadim Gushchin, in addition to his teaching responsibilities, lectured at the University of Southern Colorado and performed for a variety of classes at

Colorado College. Professor Markova lectured on mime and assisted Natal'ia Fisson and Sergei Sherbin during their highly acclaimed performances in Colorado Springs. In addition to their work with the Imagination Celebration, Ms. Fisson and Mr. Sherbin performed and spoke at Manitou Springs Elementary School, Canon Elementary School, Wasson High School, Eagleview Middle School, and appeared on KKTV. Both became honorary citizens of Colorado Springs.

[3] I have used the Library of Congress transliteration system. Familiar Russian names are anglicized.

[4] Consider the following: in 1981, the official exchange rate orchestrated by the Soviets was roughly sixty kopecks to one dollar. The black market rate was around one ruble to three dollars. In the summer of 1991, the Government exchanged rubles at a rate of about thirty-five to one. One of my students, who studied at the Herzen Institute in the fall of 1992, confirmed a rate of 475 to one. According to Fred and David Goethel, the exchange rate in St. Petersburg on June 30, 1993, was 1,072 to one. On July 1, the rate had jumped to 1,116 to one. As of this writing, Russians have until August 7 to return rubles issued prior to 1993.* On that date the older rubles will be worthless. Inflation is now running at 2,500 percent annually. See "Pre-1993 rubles to be worthless," *Reading Eagle*, 25 July 1993, p. A3. *With the exception of additional editing and later acknowledgments in the Introduction, this text was finished in the summer of 1993. Publication was subsequently delayed.

[5] The Russian questionnaire was distributed throughout 1989-90. Omissions in the questionnaire format mean that a particular question was left unanswered. The dates, when available, indicate the day when the questionnaire was filled out and recorded. A studio's repertoire is listed sequentially by author, director, and title. I have attempted, when possible, to leave the questions and answers in their original format with regard to punctuation and style. In addition, I have tried to give the titles of works known worldwide standard or established translations. Addresses and telephone numbers are provided when that information pertains to the studio itself. Otherwise, it was felt that home addresses and telephone numbers would not be appropriate for general publication. The introduction of the questionnaire is given here:

Dear Friends!

The American Council of Teachers of Russian, together with the Leningrad branch of the Union of Theater Representatives, is conducting research on the beginning and development of the studio movement in the USSR.

The researchers turn to you with the request that you answer several questions, which, as they suggest, will reveal the fundamental norms concerning the beginning of this important movement. We hope that your answers will help to create an authentic picture of the studio movement in the Soviet Union at the end of the '80s and at the beginning of the '90s, which presents genuine interest for both the American and Soviet audience.

We ask that you give the completed questionnaire to the Head Advisor at STD, Liudmila Alekseevna Korobova, at the following address: Nevsky prospekt, dom 86, STD.

We thank you for kindly agreeing to take part in our common work!

[6] Tresser's twenty-six page document is entitled *Perechen' teatral'nykh uchrezhdenii Petrograda-Leningrada za period 1917 - 1945 g.g.* Tresser has compiled another list of ninety-two "miniature" theaters which functioned in Petrograd-Leningrad from 1917-27. What is more, he writes of an additional "350 theater units, advanced theaters, theater-studios, and so on and so forth," which he has identified in archives and libraries.

[7] K. L. Rudnitskii, ed., *Sovetskii teatr* (Moskva: Iskusstvo, 1967), pp. 163-164. I have italicized the plays.

[8] Translated from Aleksandr Gladkov, *Teatr: Vospominaniia i razmyshleniia* (Moskva: Iskusstvo, 1980), pp. 269-270.

[9] In a telling echo of Meierkhol'd's sentiments, Efros discussed the role of the director: "This is a person who is capable of working joyfully. During the most serious rehearsal, even during a tragic scene, suddenly, thanks to the director everyone must be diverted to something humorous and then laugh for a long time, and then again take part in the work. But the work itself must flow along happily. 'Poetry must be silly'." Translated from Anatolii Efros, *Prodolzhenie teatral'nogo rasskaza* (Moskva: Iskusstvo, 1985), p. 155.

[10] Subbota was founded in 1969.

[11] The author wishes to thank Professor Alma Law for her helpful suggestions regarding the translation of this interview.

[12] Grotowski said, "The core of the theatre is an encounter. The man who makes an act of self-revelation is, so to speak, one who establishes contact with himself. That is to say, an extreme confrontation, sincere, disciplined, precise and total - not merely a confrontation with his thoughts, but one involving his whole being from his instincts and his unconscious right up to his most lucid state.

The theatre is also an encounter between creative people. It is myself, as a producer, who am confronted with the actor, and the self-revelation of the actor gives me a revelation of myself. The actors and myself are confronted with the text. Now, we cannot express what is objective in the text, and in fact it is only those texts which are really weak that give us a unique possibility of interpretation. All the great texts represent a sort of deep gulf for us. Take Hamlet: books without number have been devoted to this character. Professors will tell us, each for himself, that they have discovered an objective Hamlet. They suggest to us revolutionary Hamlets, rebel and impotent Hamlets, Hamlet the outsider, etc. But there is no objective Hamlet. The work is too great for that. The strength of great works really consists in their catalystic effect: they open doors for us, set in motion the machinery of our self-awareness. My encounter with the text resembles my encounter with the actor and his with me. For both producer and actor, the author's text is a sort of scalpel enabling us to open ourselves, to transcend ourselves, to find out what is hidden within us and to make the act of encountering the others; in other words, to transcend our solitude. In the theatre, if you like, the text has the same function as the myth had for the poet of ancient times." Jerzy Grotowski, *Towards a Poor Theatre* (New York: Simon and Schuster, 1968), pp. 56-57.

[13] As Marina Smyslova has pointed out, рентабельность means that the profit is sufficient for an organization to exist without donations--to pay salary, rent, and all production expenses. Прибыльность is a more general notion of everything which can provide profit.

[14] "Vakhtangov brought to the Russian theater a special kind of expressionism. In a way, his position was between the extreme of the *avant-garde* and the realistic psychologism of the Moscow Art Theater. He was not interested in experimentation for the sake of testing new devices, for he believed in the necessity of an inner truth for the actor and director. But he was greatly conscious of the particular character of theatrical reality, not to be confused with life reality, and he tried to project its organizational, and consequently esthetic, elements. What made his influence so deep and lasting was a combination of personal and professional qualities. He was not a theoretician, but was an outstanding teacher and a man completely devoted to his art. He liked people, and his friends adored him. Warmth and human understanding gave a particular glow to all his work. Many performances directed by Meyerhold or Tairov were dazzling, brilliant, absorbing, but none of them, unless they were outright tragedy, had Vakhtangov's human touch. At the same time, his productions were technically perfect, bordering on virtuosity, the result of stubborn relentless labor. Vakhtangov, who had been formed in the school of Stanislavsky and Nemirovich Danchenko, left these high standards of artistic probity as a legacy to his numerous pupils, and his name became the symbol of personal integrity. Directors and actors, such as Zavadsky, Simonov, Zakhava, Shchukin, and many others, continued his tradition and formed a whole Vakhtangov trend in the Russian theater." Marc Slonim, *Russian Theater: From the Empire to the Soviets* (Cleveland: The World Publishing Company, 1961), pp. 270-271.

[15] In a letter to Studio members and associates of November 14-15, 1918, Vakhtangov writes, "All of you joined our Studio at different times--some earlier, some later. The Studio existed before you, the Studio had its own history, dreams, and internal atmosphere before you came. Its atmosphere was friendly and enthusiastic. People came to the Studio to rest from life and to have contact with art. . . . Each group has a different sense of 'the Studio spirit' in its heart. . . . If everyone is to be equal in this respect, if everyone is to understand this notion in the same way, they must first *live the life of the Studio*; secondly, they must give of themselves to the Studio so that it becomes something near and dear to them; thirdly, when the Studio has become precious to them, then they must *defend* it against all dangers." Lyubov Vendrovskaya and Galina Kaptereva, *Evgeny Vakhtangov* (Moscow: Progress Publishers, 1982), pp. 81-82.

16"Just as only a great sinner can become a saint according to the theologians (Let us not forget the Revelation: 'So then because thou art lukewarm, and neither cold nor hot, I will spue thee out of my mouth'), in the same way the actor's wretchedness can be transformed into a kind of holiness. The history of the theatre has numerous examples of this.

Don't get me wrong. I speak about 'holiness' as an unbeliever. I mean a 'secular holiness'. If the actor, by setting himself a challenge publicly challenges others, and through excess, profanation and outrageous sacrilege reveals himself by casting off his everyday mask, he makes it possible for the spectator to undertake a similar process of self-penetration. If he does not exhibit his body, but annihilates it, burns it, frees it from every resistance to any psychic impulse, then he does not sell his body but sacrifices it. He repeats the atonement; he is close to holiness. If such acting is not to be something transient and fortuitous, a phenomenon which cannot be foreseen in time or space: if we want a theatre group whose daily bread is this kind of work - then we must follow a special method of research and training" (Grotowski, p. 34).

17I am very grateful to Professor Omry Ronen of the University of Michigan for identifying these lines. Actually, the quotation is from a letter Blok wrote to his wife on February 19, 1915: "узорные финтифлюшки вокруг пустынной души." Thus, a translation could read, "Patterned bagatelles (knick-knacks) around an empty soul." Professor Ronen indicates that the phrase is often misquoted as indicated with Sasha Maslov's "Будут красивые финтифлюшки, а вокруг пустынные души." Ironically, in the very same letter Blok refers to his attendance at a play staged by Meierkhol'd's studio. See Aleksandr Blok, *Pis'ma k zhene*, tom 89 of *Literaturnoe nasledstvo* (Moskva: Nauka, 1978), pp. 353-354.

18Eduard Bersudskii has crafted the various statues and puppets at Sharmanka.

19"Just as any doctor does not necessarily make a good psychiatrist, not any producer can succeed in this form of theatre. The principle to apply as a piece of advice, and also a warning, is the following: 'Primum non nocere' ('First, do not harm'). To express this in technical language: it is better to suggest by means of sound and gesture than to 'act' in front of the actor or supply him with intellectual explanations; better to express oneself by means of a silence or a wink of the eye than by instructions, observing the stages in the psychological breakdown and collapse of the actor in order then to come to his aid. One must be strict, but like a father or older brother. The second principle is one common to all professions: if you make demands on your colleagues, you must make twice as many demands on yourself" (Grotowski, pp. 47-48).

20Pavel Aleksandrovich Florenskii was a "Russian theologian, philosopher, and scientist, and a leading figure in the development of the twentieth-century Russian religious philosophy inspired by Vladimir Solovyov." See Paul Edwards, ed., *The Encyclopedia of Philosophy*, vol. 3 (New York: The Macmillan Company, 1967), p. 205.

[21]Райисполком is defined as the District Executive Committee while Испонительный комитет is the Executive Committee.

[22]"Stanislavsky's method aimed at an inner discipline of the actor, at the highest degree of artistic intelligence and at a perfect control of all external means. It is obvious that such a method did not deny the importance of natural talent but simply tried to develop it through a rigorous discipline of work, study, experiment, and conscious effort. We should not forget that Stanislavsky always had in mind the super-objective as the supreme goal of a performance: 'to convey the emotions and the ideas of a playwright, his dreams, torments, and joys'. The trunkline or through action mobilizes all the psychic and physical efforts of the actor and gives consistency to the whole work, including its form, in settings, lighting, and structure of the stage. The unity of the physical and of the inner psychogical is the key to the success of the whole--for a total production as well as the rendition of a part by an individual actor" (Slonim, p. 166).

[23]In the spring of 1905 ". . . Stanislavsky and Meierkhol'd began a new project with great enthusiasm. Their ideas, as Stanislavsky recalled, 'demanded a preliminary laboratory of work. It is not a place in the theater with daily productions, with complicated demands and a strictly calculated budget. Some kind of special establishment is needed which Vsevolod Emil'evich has successfully called a *teatral'naia studiia*. This is not a prepared theater or a school for beginners, but a laboratory for the experiments of more or less experienced actors.'" Translated from K. L. Rudnitskii, *Rezhisser Meierkhol'd* (Moskva: Nauka, 1968), p. 49. Stanislavsky's quote is from K. S. Stanislavskogo, *Sobranie sochinenii*, tom 1 (Moskva: Iskusstvo, 1954), p. 186.

[24]"The Moscow Art Theater was like a symphonic orchestra under a brilliant conductor. It had no soloists and its unity was essentially that of a highly professional team. Its opponents called it the theater of directors and claimed that the actor was sacrificed to the smoothness of the ensemble work. The accusation was, however, unjust: to achieve the miracle of co-operation and harmony, the Theater needed first-class actors, and as we know, Stanislavsky directed his main efforts toward the training of each individual member of his company. He and Nemirovich Danchenko succeeded in assembling a group of men and women out of which, at one time or another, emerged all the best Russian actors and actresses of the twentieth century. Some of them, such as Meyerhold or Vakhtangov or Mikhail Chekhov, later broke away from the institution which had been their alma mater, but others remained loyal to it all their lives. And of course, Stanislavsky himself was an excellent and highly talented actor" (Slonim, p. 167).

[25]"At the end of December, 1913, a group of students invited Vakhtangov to direct Boris Zaitsev's play, *The Lanin Estate*. The play was premiered March 26, 1914, but was not a success. However, the amateurs who had gathered around Vakhtangov decided not to disband and to devote their free time to serious theatrical studies. That is how the Student Studio came into being (from 1917 on it

was called The Vakhtangov Drama Studio). In the autumn of 1920 the Studio was incorporated into the Moscow Art Theatre as the Third Art Theatre Studio, and after 1926 it became known as the Vakhtangov Theatre" (Vendrovskaya and Kaptereva, p. 63).

[26]The Sovremennik came into being in 1955 with official approval. "Here, a group of young actors under equally youthful leadership staged new Soviet plays which stressed a need to value human feeling and to cherish the significance of personality and individuality within a collective context.... the way was led by Oleg Efremov at the Sovremennik, who staged seminal productions of important British and American plays. The plays of Tennessee Williams, Arthur Miller and Edward Albee began to establish themselves as standard components of the Soviet repertoire. Brecht, whose work had first been staged by Tairov in 1930, but who had since been allowed to lapse into oblivion, was rediscovered and given vivid and imaginative productions by Yuri Lyubimov at the revitalised Theatre of Drama and Comedy on Taganka Square." Nick Worral, *Modernism to Realism on the Soviet Stage* (Cambridge: Cambridge University Press, 1989), pp. 13-14.

[27]An enactment by the Ministry of Culture and STD of the USSR regarding the transfer of theater-studios to new conditions of organizational, creative, and economic activity went into effect on March 16, 1989.

[28]The Soiuz teatral'nykh deiatelei (STD) is the Theater Union located in the Stanislavsky Actors' Home on Nevsky prospekt.

[29]See Part III for the list of theater-studios revised by M. A. Naimark of the Leningrad State Institute of Theater, Music, and Cinematography.

[30]Oliver M. Sayler was aware of differences between Moscow and Petrograd in 1918 when he wrote, "Meyerhold and Yevreynoff, --these were the two names that lured me from the comparative safety of Moscow to the uncertainties of Petrograd during those anxious days of February, 1918, when the gray hordes of the Germans were swarming on unimpeded toward the capital. The stages of Moscow are the Russian theatre in microcosm, --with two exceptions.... No one in Moscow could deny it, no matter how partisan was his interest in his own city's playhouses. The exceptions were so exceptional that their fame had travelled before the war to far-off America alongside that of Stanislavsky and the Art Theatre and the Ballet. Meyerhold stood out in these rumors as the uncompromising foe of Stanislavsky and realism, the defender and practitioner of the theatre theatrical. Yevreynoff emerged dimly in the guise of a proponent of a new way of conceiving the theatre, monodrama. From my first consultation with Tardoff and my first visit to Stanislavsky's dressing room, these two names were spoken with respect wherever Russian artists gathered. Under the spell of the Moscow theatres, I had lingered in the Kremlin city almost four months. But a visit to Petrograd was essential, Germans or no Germans!" Oliver M. Sayler, *The Russian Theatre* (New York: Brentano's Publishers, 1922), pp. 202-203. Sharon Marie Carnicke writes that Evreinov "... was working in a vacuum, searching for a new vocabulary for theatre

when his contemporaries were not. In this respect he was ahead of his time. Modern directors--such as Peter Brook who toured Africa looking for the roots of theatre in non-verbal communication, Grotowski who created a new kind of ritual theatre, . . . unknowingly echo Evreinov's thinking if not his aesthetic principles." Sharon Marie Carnicke, *The Theatrical Instinct: Nikolai Evreinov and the Russian Theatre of the Early Twentieth Century* (New York: Peter Lang, 1989), p. 5.

[31] Tovstonogov wrote, "I was born too late to become his pupil. I studied the plays and productions by Konstantin Sergeevich [Stanislavsky]; studied, looking at the actors raised by him, studied with those whom he taught and in whom he believed." Translated from G. Tovstonogov, *Zerkalo stseny: O professii rezhissera* (Leningrad: Iskusstvo, 1980), p. 35.

[32] VOTM (Всероссийское объединение: Творческие мастерские) is the All-Russian Association of Creative Studios.

[33] The Road (Doroga) later became the Leningrad Chamber Theater.

[34] Ironically, Vakhtangov would hold over two hundred rehearsals for a production staged three or four times a year. By making *Princess Turandot*, a play derived from the fairy tale by Carlos Gozzi, "a celebration of merriment and wit, Vakhtangov created a contrast to the gloominess of the times, and his colorful joyful art exploded in the dark Moscow of 1921 as a challenge to the ascetic productions of Meyerhold and the abstract logic of Tairov. The night of the *Turandot* dress rehearsal Vakhtangov felt very ill; he had a temperature of 102°, but he continued to direct and correct, and sat in the theater for hours, muffled up in a fur coat, a wet towel around his head. After that night he could not get up from his bed, and he only heard of the tremendous success of his beloved *Turandot*: he was too sick to go to the performance. He died thee months later" (Slonim, p. 270).

[35] This word means self-publishing.

[36] *Nemaia stsena* is Sergei Dreiden's one-man interpretation of Gogol's *The Inspector General*.

[37] Sadly enough, a fire later gutted Leningrad VOTM's headquarters. The organization was then disbanded.

[38] Grotowski said, "We do not cater for the man who goes to the theatre to satisfy a social need for contact with culture: in other words, to have something to talk about to his friends and to be able to say that he has seen this or that play and that it was interesting. We are not there to satisfy his 'cultural needs'. This is cheating.
Nor do we cater for the man who goes to the theatre to relax after a hard day's work. Everyone has a right to relax after work and there are numerous forms of entertainment for this purpose, ranging from certain types of film to cabaret and music-hall, and many more on the same lines.

We are concerned with the spectator who has genuine spiritual needs and who really wishes, through confrontation with the performance to analyse himself. We are concerned with the spectator who does not stop at an elementary stage of psychic integration, content with his own petty, geometrical, spiritual stability, knowing exactly what is good and what is evil, and never in doubt. For it was not to him that El Greco, Norwid, Thomas Mann and Dostoevsky spoke, but to him who undergoes an endless process of self-development, whose unrest is not general but directed towards a search for the truth about himself and his mission in life" (Grotowski, p. 40).

[39]"We cannot know whether the theatre is still necessary today since all social attractions, entertainments, form and colour effects have been taken over by film and television. Everybody repeats the same rhetorical question: is the theatre necessary? But we only ask it in order to be able to reply: yes, it is, because it is an art which is always young and always necessary. The sale of performances is organized on a grand scale. Yet no one organizes film and television audiences in the same way. If all theatres were closed down one day, a large percentage of the people would know nothing about it until weeks later, but if one were to eliminate cinemas and television, the very next day the whole population would be in an uproar. Many theatre people are conscious of this problem, but hit upon the wrong solution: since the cinema dominates theatre from a technical point of view, why not make the theatre more technical? . . . The theatre must recognize its own limitations. If it cannot be richer than the cinema, then let it be poor. If it cannot be as lavish as television, let it be ascetic. If it cannot be a technical attraction, let it renounce all outward technique. Thus we are left with a 'holy' actor in a poor theatre" (Grotowski, p. 41).

[40]"The poor theatre does not offer the actor the possibility of overnight success. It defies the bourgeois concept of a standard of living. It proposes the substitution of material wealth by moral wealth as the principal aim in life. Yet who does not cherish a secret wish to rise to sudden affluence? This too may cause opposition and negative reactions, even if these are not clearly formulated. Work in such an ensemble can never be stable. It is nothing but a huge challenge and, furthermore, it awakens such strong reactions of aversion that these often threaten the theatre's very existence" (Grotowski, pp. 44-45).

[41]As a non-native speaker of Russian, I rely on Marina Smyslova's explanation of the difference between истина and правда. She writes, "I think истина is a more fundamental philosophical notion. It's a more profound truth. Правда has more to do with particular cases. Also, supposedly истина means the only one. . . . Sometimes they mean the same in context. Истина is used to strengthen, to stress the meaning."

[42]In 1968 M. Iankovskii wrote that "The Theater of Comedy has long since ceased to be a Leningrad phenomenon alone. As a rule, it completes each season in different cities of the country. It is a frequent guest in Moscow, it travels abroad, and everywhere is met with a warm response. And, of course, at the same time, it

provokes arguments." Translated from M. O. Iankovskii, *Leningradskii teatr komedii* (Leningrad: Iskusstvo, 1968), p. 177.

[43] A *kapustnik* is an evening of sketches and songs understandable to people of a certain professional or artistic milieu.

[44] Liudmila Petrushevskaia is a popular contemporary playwright in St. Petersburg.

[45] This was the Belgrade Festival of Experimental Theaters.

[46] According to Marino Deseilligny of the University of Washington with regard to plot summaries of Anouilh's plays, "None of these jump at me as a play which could be translated as Генералы в юбках. However, it is conceivable that the play on Joan of Arc (*L'Alouette*) be called that. Or perhaps it could be *L'Hurluberu*. . . ." The plot summary of the latter play reads: "The hero, a retired general, hates the postwar world, wants France to return to more conservative ways, and plots to overthrow the existing regime. He is confused and does not understand himself or those around him. He loves his young wife but is afraid that she is faithful to him only through a sense of duty. Like Alceste, the General is his own worst enemy and suffers defeat after defeat but remains unconquered." See Kathleen White Kelly, *Jean Anouilh: An Annotated Bibliography* (Metuchen: The Scarecrow Press, 1973), p. 86.

[47] "Крошка сын к отцу пришел" is from Vladimir Mayakovsky's poem "What is Good and What is Bad?" (*"Chto takoe khorosho i chto takoe plokho?"*).

[48] All interviews were recorded with a small hand-held tape recorder.

[49] The premiere of Lermontov's *Masquerade* directed by Meierkhol'd at the Aleksandrinskii Theater took place on February 25, 1917. Meierkhol'd revived the play in 1938.

[50] Vakhtangov wrote the following in his notebook on October 22, 1918:
"The actor's education must consist in enriching his subconscious mind with a diversity of abilities: an ability to be free, be concentrated, be serious, scenic, artistic, effective, expressive, observant, quick to adapt, and so on. Such abilities are endless.
The subconscious mind, armed with such a reserve of means, will fashion a virtually perfect work out of the material it receives.
Essentially, the actor should only have to study and assimilate the text, together with his partners, and go on to the stage to create his part.
This is the ideal. When the actor has been trained in all the necessary abilities. The actor must, without fail, improvise. This is what talent means. God knows what goes on in theatrical schools. The schools' main mistake is that they try to *teach*, instead of *educating*" (Vendrovskaya, p. 122).

⁵¹DK stands for *Dvorets kul'tury* or Palace of Culture. ZHEK is short for *Zhilishchno-eksplutatsionnaia kontora,* a rental office and REU is the abbreviation for *Raionnoe eksplutatsionnoe upravlenie,* a larger and more updated version of ZHEK.

⁵²Baron Anton Antonovich Del'vig (1798-1831) belonged to the Pushkin Pleiad of Russian poets.

⁵³Vakhtangov recorded the following in his notebook on April 15, 1911:
"I want to form a studio where we could study. The principle would be to do everything by ourselves. Everyone would be a director. We would test Stanislavsky's Method on ourselves. We would either accept or refute it, correct it, add to it, or take what is false out of it. Everyone who enters the studio should love art in general and the theatre in particular. They should search for joy in art. They should forget about the audience and create for themselves. They should enjoy what they are doing for themselves, be their own judges. I'd like to introduce lessons in mime, voice training, and fencing from the very beginning. Lectures on the history of art and costume. Once a week we should listen to music (invite musicians). Each would bring here whatever comes to his head, everything interesting he can think of: jokes, music, short plays" (Vendrovskaya, p. 13).

⁵⁴"Can the theatre exist without costumes and seats? Yes, it can.
Can it exist without music to accompany the plot? Yes.
Can it exist without lighting effects? Of course.
And without a text? Yes; the history of the theatre confirms this. In the evolution of the theatrical art the text was one of the last elements to be added. If we place some people on a stage with a scenario they themselves have put together and let improvise their parts as in the Commedia dell'Arte, the performance will be equally good even if the words are not articulated but simply muttered" (Grotowski, p. 32).

⁵⁵Vakhtangov said the following, "And when you spectators realized that they're on the wrong path, you stopped reacting to what was going on before you. You must react, act and live as spectators do when they watch a play. . . . And why do the actors like to hear the audience laugh? Why doesn't it disturb them? What are you afraid of? That you'll not win the audience? If you can't, you're no actor, just a dilettante. In that case, go and play charades at your friends' birthday parties." Nikolai Gorchakov, *The Vakhtangov School of Stage Art* (Moscow: Foreign Language Publishing House, 195-?), p. 122.

⁵⁶Historically in Russia the *skomorokhi* were traveling minstrels and comedians often in conflict with religious authorities. The plight of one such medieval performer is depicted in several scenes from Tarkovsky's *Andrei Rublev.*

⁵⁷The term certainly has some historical resonance. Note that Evreinov's production of *The Inspector General* was entitled *Revizor, rezhisserskaia buffonada* (Carnicke, p. 32). Bulgakov, in 1926, called the genre of his *Zoyka's Apartment*

tragicheskaia buffonada or "tragic buffonade."   Lesley Milne, "Mikhail Bulgakov: the Status of the Dramatist and the Status of the Text," *Russian Theatre in the Age of Modernism*, eds., Robert Russell and Andrew Barratt (New York: St. Martin's Press, 1990), p. 239.

[58]"The monopoly of the Imperial Theaters created a peculiar situation in the second half of the nineteenth century: the whole style and repertory of the Russian stage depended on what was going on in Moscow and St. Petersburg. Private theatrical enterprises did exist legally in the provinces, but in the two capitals they could come to life only under disguise or in very devious ways paved by huge bribes. Usually amateurs, or even professionals, performed in clubs and at so-called family reunions. Some performances were given under the auspices of the Circle of Lovers of Dramatic Art, established in Moscow in 1861. In St. Petersburg, many plays were produced at 'dramatic evenings' at the Nobility Assembly (which possessed a good stage) and at the Painters or Merchants Clubs. Summer stock theaters and operettas had no difficulty in obtaining special licenses. In any case, by the middle of the seventies there were some twenty-five theatrical ventures (not including the Imperial Theaters) functioning fairly regularly in Moscow and St. Petersburg. This meant that the monopoly lost its political justification--especially in the light of the huge development of theaters in the provinces and the number of companies on the road which often included prominent artists. Under the pressure of public opinion and a few enlightened men of the theatrical administration, among them Ostrovsky, the government decided to legalize the existing conditions and to abolish the monopoly" (Slonim, p. 84).

PART II

QUESTIONNAIRES

The Theater of the Absurd (Театр абсурда)
4/19/90

1. When was your collective officially registered in accordance with the regulations for theater-studios?

May 1988

2. When was your first production performed?

At which institution was your theater-studio registered?

b) The Youth Culture Center (Vasileostrovskii Youth Center)

In what capacity did you exist prior to registration?

3. Name the productions in your repertoire [Author, Director, Play]:

A. Gunitskii   M. Gindin   *The Death of the Ticketless*

4. If possible, please formulate the creative credo of your studio and the principles of your association (the creative, organizational, commercial, and humane goals)

The verdict of realistic art which is carried out. The word has ceased to function. We do not hear each other at all. Let's destroy the chain of formal logic. Or, having ears, let's hear everything. That's all and amen.

5. How many people are in your collective today? 12

Men: 8

Women: 4

younger than 25 years: 3

from 26 to 35: 9

How many people have a theater education? 5

6. What are the average earnings of the actors in your studio?

On an average 200 rubles.

7. Do you have your own rehearsal space?

c) No, we have to rehearse wherever we can

9. By what means do you prepare decorations, costumes, props, and so forth?

a) We order them from an artistic staging complex

10. Do you have a special permanent location for the storage of your props?

b) We do not have a special location, but use the rehearsal space at other locations

11. Do you have a permanent location for the run of a production? No

15. How many presentations did your studio give in 1989? 60 productions

    at other locations:

    in Leningrad: 10 productions

    on tour: 50 productions

16. How many spectators attended productions in your studio in 1989?

Approximately 40,000 spectators

Of this number 37,000 spectators on tour

17. What is the average price of a ticket to a production at your theater?

On tour 2.5 rubles

18. What problems did you run into as your studio came into being?

A lack of support from those in power, a lack of money, and location.

19. What most of all worries you and alarms you at the present time?

Mentioned above

20. In your opinion, how could government and societal organizations show support for you?

Mentioned above

21. In your opinion, what is the central problem in the life of your studio?

An indifference of the State to the problems of the theater.

22. In your opinion, what is the central problem in the life of contemporary Soviet theater?

Mentioned above

Arena (Арена)
4/4/90

1. When was your collective officially registered in accordance with the regulations for theater-studios?

November 1988

2. When was your first production performed?

December 1988

At which institution was your theater-studio registered?

d) At the Palace of Culture of Railway Men

In what capacity did you exist prior to registration?

As a people's theater

3. Name the productions in your repertoire:

F. G. Lorca	N. N. Pereviazko	*The Spanish Ballad*
O. Tumanian	A. S. Nikulin	*A Drop of Honey*
A. S. Pushkin	A. S. Nikulin	*Mozart and Salieri* (incl. *The Feast During the Plague*)
A. S. Pushkin	A. S. Nikulin	*The Tale About the Tsar Saltan*
A. S. Pushkin	A. S. Nikulin	*The Tale About the Priest and His Workman Balda*
I. Tokmakova	A. S. Nikulin	*The Winter's Tale*

4. If possible, please formulate the creative credo of your studio and the principles of your association (the creative, organizational, commercial, and humane goals)

An organic union on the basis of the dramatic action of dance, movement, music, singing
Current affairs and the principles of the studio

5. How many people are in your collective today? 22

Men: 8

Women: 12

younger than 25 years: 12

from 26 to 35: 8

QUESTIONNAIRES

from 36 to 45: 1

from 46 to 55: 1

How many people have a theater education? 6

6. What are the average earnings of the actors in your studio?

On an average 120 rubles.

7. Do you have your own rehearsal space?

a) Yes, we have our own

d) Other: But other collectives work at this location

8. What are the dimensions of the rehearsal space which you use?

100 m^2

9. By what means do you prepare decorations, costumes, props, and so forth?

b) We use what we have

d) We prepare them ourselves

10. Do you have a special permanent location for the storage of your props?

b) We do not have a special location, but use the rehearsal space or other locations

11. Do you have a permanent location for the run of a production? No

12. What is real capacity of your hall? 100

13. What is the usual attendance? 80

14. Was it necessary for you to re-equip this location?

c) We essentially had to re-equip the location

What was accommodated at your location before it was given to the theater?

A choreography class

15. How many presentations did your studio give in 1989? 200 productions

　　　　at your own location: 15 productions

at other locations:

in Leningrad: 165 productions

on tour: 20 productions

16. How many spectators attended productions in your studio in 1989?

Approximately 40,000 spectators

Of this number 6,000 spectators on tour

17. What is the average price of a ticket to a production at your theater?

At the permanent location 1 ruble

On tour 2 rubles

18. What problems did you run into as your studio came into being?

The main problem is the lack of our own location
A lack of attention from the theater critics
The lack of a financial base

19. What most of all worries you and alarms you at the present time?

The problems enumerated in question 18
The weak theater culture of the audience

20. In your opinion, how could government and societal organizations show support for you?

Help in solving the problems stated in question 18

21. In your opinion, what is the central problem in the life of your studio?

The lack of a sponsor

22. In your opinion, what is the central problem in the life of contemporary Soviet theater?

The decline of theater culture
It is difficult to answer this question in two words

QUESTIONNAIRES

The Leningrad Chamber Theater
(Ленинградский камерный театр)
4/2/90

1. When was your collective officially registered in accordance with the regulations for theater-studios?

December 1989

2. When was your first production performed?

November 1988

At which institution was your theater-studio registered?

a) The Culture Administration; Smol'ninskii Raiispolkom

In what capacity did you exist prior to registration?

In the capacity of a theater-studio at the Youth Cultural Center of the Smol'ninskii Regional Komsomol Committee.

3. Name the productions in your repertoire:

Plastic Fantasies based on the theme of ancient Japanese poetry	V. Koifman	*The Stone Garden*
Albee	V. Koifman	*Zoo Story*
Beckett	V. Koifman	*Endspiel*
Durrenmatt	V. Koifman	*Play Strindberg*
	V. Koifman	*Clown Mime Show*
	V. Koifman	*Crazy Fantasy*
Harris	V. Koifman	*The Uncle Remus Tales*

4. If possible, please formulate the creative credo of your studio and the principles of your association (the creative, organizational, commercial, and humane goals)

The theater is the way to each other. The person is always at the center of attention, the life of the human spirit.
The principles of unification--professionalism and the idea of the studio. Commerce is the second plan, only as a means of existence.

5. How many people are in your collective today? 20

Men: 15

QUESTIONNAIRES

Women: 5

younger than 25 years: 4

from 26 to 35: 16

How many people have a theater education? 9

6. What are the average earnings of the actors in your studio?

On an average 100 rubles.

7. Do you have your own rehearsal space?

b) No, we rent a permanent location

8. What are the dimensions of the rehearsal space which you use?

45 m^2

9. By what means do you prepare decorations, costumes, props, and so forth?

a) We order them from an artistic staging complex

b) We use what we have

d) We prepare them ourselves

10. Do you have a special permanent location for the storage of your props?

b) We do not have a special location, but use the rehearsal space or other locations

11. Do you have a permanent location for the run of a production? Yes

12. What is real capacity of your hall? 100

13. What is the usual attendance? 70

14. Was it necessary for you to re-equip this location?

c) We essentially had to re-equip the location

What was accommodated at your location before it was given to the theater?

Women's consultation service

15. How many presentations did your studio give in 1989? 100 productions

at your own location: 50 productions

at other locations: 50

in Leningrad: 80 productions

on tour: 20 productions

16. How many spectators attended productions in your studio in 1989?

Approximately 10,000 spectators

Of this number 2,000 spectators on tour

17. What is the average price of a ticket to a production at your theater?

At the permanent location 2.5 rubles

On tour 1 ruble

18. What problems did you run into as your studio came into being?

Financial problems connected with the stage areas.

19. What most of all worries you and alarms you at the present time?

See 18.

20. In your opinion, how could government and societal organizations show support for you?

By [giving] more attention to the work of the collective, financial support, and by granting a location for work.

21. In your opinion, what is the central problem in the life of your studio?*

22. In your opinion, what is the central problem in the life of contemporary Soviet theater?

Your address: Leningrad, ul. Bakunina 2
Telephone: 274-01-46

*Questions 21 and 22 were not answered as many members of the troupe were touring Europe at the time.

QUESTIONNAIRES

Beyond the Black River (За черной речкой)
2/11/90

1. When was your collective officially registered in accordance with the regulations for theater-studios?

April 1983

2. When was your first production performed?

March 1983

At which institution was your theater-studio registered?

b) The Youth Culture Center; Primorskii District

d) Culture Section of the Primorskii District

In what capacity did you exist prior to registration?

As an amateur collective without a State funding

3. Name the productions in your repertoire:

Iurii Tynianov, M. Tsvetaeva	Mendel'son	*Students of the Lycee*
Peter Weiss	Abramov	*The Inquest*
Lewis Carroll	Abramov	*Through the Looking Glass*
Foreign Novellas	Eroshin	*In Our Time*
Ia. Rainis	Mendel'son	*Blow Little Wind*
R. Katz	Mendel'son	*The Turning Point*
R. Katz	Mendel'son	*In Memory of a Teacher*
R. Katz	Mendel'son	*Tili-tili-testo*
R. Katz	Mendel'son	*Ul'ul'um*
Sergienko	Eroshin	*Farewell Ravine*
Zimin	Mendel'son	*Shoo!*
Mayakovsky	Mendel'son	*The Left-Wing Forward!*
B. Goller	Mendel'son	*The Myth about Commandos*

5. How many people are in your collective today? 25

Men: 17

Women: 8

younger than 25 years: 25

6. What are the average earnings of the actors in your studio?

On an average 100 rubles.

7. Do you have your own rehearsal space?

a) Yes, we have our own

8. What are the dimensions of the rehearsal space which you use?

100 m^2

9. By what means do you prepare decorations, costumes, props, and so forth?

a) We order them from an artistic staging complex

d) We prepare them ourselves

10. Do you have a special permanent location for the storage of your props?

a) Yes

11. Do you have a permanent location for the run of a production? Yes

12. What is real capacity of your hall? 100

13. What is the usual attendance? 100

14. Was it necessary for you to re-equip this location?

c) We essentially had to re-equip the location

What was accommodated at your location before it was given to the theater?

A high school

15. How many presentations did your studio give in 1989? 122 productions

       at your own location: 87

       at other locations: 35 productions

       in Leningrad: 122 productions

16. How many spectators attended productions in your studio in 1989?

Approximately 12,000 spectators

17. What is the average price of a ticket to a production at your theater?

At the permanent location 1 ruble

On tour 1.5 rubles

18. What problems did you run into as your studio came into being?

A lack of interest on the part of local government officials in the development of the studio movement. Financial self-support and the fact we only have what we take in.

19. What most of all worries you and alarms you at the present time?

a) The absence of the prospect of development
b) The prospect of losing the location
c) A lack of sponsors who would subsidize [us].

20. In your opinion, how could government and societal organizations show support for you?

Moral and material support

21. In your opinion, what is the central problem in the life of your studio?

The problem of survival and problem of creative experimentation

22. In your opinion, what is the central problem in the life of contemporary Soviet theater?

The spectators have been torn away, commercialized art, and the impossibility of experimentation in the professional theater.

Your address: Leningrad, pos. Kolom'agi, 3-aia liniia, dom 10a
Telephone: 395-34-02

QUESTIONNAIRES 103

Da-Net (Да-нет)
4/12/90

1. When was your collective officially registered in accordance with the regulations for theater-studios?

December 25, 1987

At which institution was your theater-studio registered?

b) The Youth Culture Center (Vyborgskii District, up to June, 1989)

d) Since August 1989, the theater has existed at the Society for the Encouragement of Contemporary Art, "A-Ia." Founder: Presidium of the Academy of Sciences of the USSR and the Moscow News

In what capacity did you exist prior to registration?

The director, the stage artist, and two actresses ran the children's theater, "Da-da-da" of the Vyborgskii District. The actress Vikulina directed the adult troupe at the Lensovet Palace of Culture. From 1981 to 1983--a private troupe.

3. Name the productions in your repertoire:

A. Vvedenskii (poem)	B. Ponizovskii	*About What (The Puppy and the Kitten)*
Actors' Composition	Performance-Project	*The Language of Farce from Theatrical Silence*
M. Betsuyaku*	A. Anferov	*100 Yen for the Service*
A. Strindberg	B. Ponizovskii	*Miss Julie*
E. Kuzmina-Karavaeva	B. Ponizovskii	*Anna*
I. Brodsky	B. Ponizovskii	*Marble*
C. Perrault	B. Ponizovskii	*Where are You?*
Comp. of stage artists and actors		*Lies about How the Varangians on the Way to the Greeks Fell in with the Slavs*
Iu. Volkov	B. Ponizovskii	*Penelope***
G. Verga	B. Ponizovskii	*She-Wolf***
A. Pushkin	B. Ponizovskii	*The Little Tragedies***

4. If possible, please formulate the creative credo of your studio and the principles of your association (the creative, organizational, commercial, and humane goals)

The actors are the authors: a theater of variations involving the actor, objects, and puppets
An association of mutual interests towards the ideas of the stage artists, directors, and the improvisation of the actors.

5. How many people are in your collective today? 15

Men: 7

Women: 8

younger than 25 years: 7

from 26 to 35: 5

from 36 to 45: 2

older than 56: 1

How many people have a theater education? 9

6. What are the average earnings of the actors in your studio?

On an average 120 rubles.

7. Do you have your own rehearsal space?

b) No, we rent a permanent location

8. What are the dimensions of the rehearsal space which you use?

60 m^2

9. By what means do you prepare decorations, costumes, props, and so forth?

a) We order them from an artistic staging complex

b) We use what we have

d) We prepare them ourselves

10. Do you have a special permanent location for the storage of your props?

a) Yes, for the time being

11. Do you have a permanent location for the run of a production? No

12. What is real capacity of your hall? Up to 300

13. What is the usual attendance? 150-200

What was accommodated at your location before it was given to the theater?

A communal apartment

15. How many presentations did your studio give in 1989? 100 productions

   at other locations

   in Leningrad: 100 productions

16. How many spectators attended productions in your studio in 1989?

Approximately from 900 to 1200 spectators

17. What is the average price of a ticket to a production at your theater?

At the permanent location 1.5 rubles

18. What problems did you run into as your studio came into being?

Zero administration; a lack of a location

19. What most of all worries you and alarms you at the present time?

The worry about the location which exists [we have]. The creation of an administration

20. In your opinion, how could government and societal organizations show support for you?

To give a permanent basement

21. In your opinion, what is the central problem in the life of your studio?

The cultivation of a discovered language.

22. In your opinion, what is the central problem in the life of contemporary Soviet theater?

The definition of individuality

*On the original questionnaire Minoru Betsuyaku was listed as B. Minoru. I am very grateful to Natsu Tabata of the Bryn Mawr College Educational Exchange Program for her help in correctly identifying the author.

**One-Man Show

QUESTIONNAIRES

The Twelve (Двенадцать)
2/15/90

1. When was your collective officially registered in accordance with the regulations for theater-studios?

1987

2. When was your first production performed?

1987

At which institution was your theater-studio registered?

d) The Komsomol Committee at the Kirov Factory

In what capacity did you exist prior to registration?

We did not exist.

3. Name the productions in your repertoire:

No. And in general this questionnaire should be sent to a humor magazine.

4. If possible, please formulate the creative credo of your studio and the principles of your association (the creative, organizational, commercial, and humane goals)

The attempt at self-realization

5. How many people are in your collective today?

At present, no one.

7. Do you have your own rehearsal space?

b) No, we rent a permanent location

9. By what means do you prepare decorations, costumes, props, and so forth?

a) We order them from an artistic staging complex

10. Do you have a special permanent location for the storage of your props?

c) No, the props are kept in the apartments of the studio members

11. Do you have a permanent location for the run of a production? No

19. What most of all worries you and alarms you at the present time?

a) the lack of any kind of support from someone (in particular from all levels of city government)

b) the lack of a rehearsal location and a location for the storage of decorations and props

c) the lack of financial means

20. In your opinion, how could government and societal organizations show support for you?

By means of a mass exit towards a pension or retirement.

21. In your opinion, what is the central problem in the life of your studio?

The impossibility to begin work.

22. In your opinion, what is the central problem in the life of contemporary Soviet theater?

The general conditions of life (the unpreparedness of broad levels of the public to the use of culture). The lack of a demand or calling for culture.

QUESTIONNAIRES

The Verb-Word (Глагол)

1. When was your collective officially registered in accordance with the regulations for theater-studios?

March 1985 (title of people's amateur theater)

2. When was your first production performed?

April 1971

At which institution was your theater-studio registered?

d) The M. I. Kalinin Leningrad Polytechnic Institute Club

In what capacity did you exist prior to registration?

A student theater of the Physics-Metallurgical Department

3. Name the productions in your repertoire:

L. Filatov	K. Gershov	*About Fedot the Strelets-the Daring Fellow*
The theater collective	E. Levitskii	*The Course of Study*
L. Petrushevskaia	K. Gershov	*Love*

4. If possible, please formulate the creative credo of your studio and the principles of your association (the creative, organizational, commercial, and humane goals)

Every person is talented. There isn't anyone who is not gifted. The theater is the way to spiritual self-perfection, the possibility of the public expression of one's civic and humane position. The professionalization of amateurism is a fallacious path (this has been proven many times by the practical experience of Soviet amateur theater).

5. How many people are in your collective today? 35

Men: 15

Women: 20

younger than 25 years: 29

from 26 to 35: 6

How many people have a theater education? 0

6. What are the average earnings of the actors in your studio?

On an average 0 rubles.

7. Do you have your own rehearsal space?

a) Yes, we have our own

8. What are the dimensions of the rehearsal space which you use?

70 m^2

9. By what means do you prepare decorations, costumes, props, and so forth?

d) We prepare them ourselves

10. Do you have a special permanent location for the storage of your props?

a) Yes

11. Do you have a permanent location for the run of a production? No

15. How many presentations did your studio give in 1989? 36 productions

>   at your own location (club): 6 productions

>   at other locations

>   in Leningrad: 21 productions

>   on tour: 9 productions

16. How many spectators attended productions in your studio in 1989?

Approximately 7,000 spectators

Of this number 2,000 spectators on tour

18. What problems did you run into as your studio came into being?

The paradox of amateurism: the participation in a production of the maximum number of the collective's participants which personally hampered the running of the production.

Money

19. What most of all worries you and alarms you at the present time?

The political and economic destabilization of the situation in the country. The real possibility of a military overthrow.
The decline of people's human dignity, the loss of faith in anything.
The dehumanization of society.

20. In your opinion, how could government and societal organizations show support for you?

By a return to the system of subsidizing the non-professional collectives, which is practically already impossible.

21. In your opinion, what is the central problem in the life of your studio?

The impossibility of stable work in the conditions of financial self-support.
The lack of our own location.

22. In your opinion, what is the central problem in the life of contemporary Soviet theater?

The lack of the audience's trust and interest in the theater, because of the situation in which it exists at present.
The demand for a search by the theater of new ways of development, of a qualitatively new status.

QUESTIONNAIRES

The Globe (Глобус)
4/10/90

1. When was your collective officially registered in accordance with the regulations for theater-studios?

June 1988

2. When was your first production performed?

June 1988

At which institution was your theater-studio registered?

d) The October Center of Youth Initiative

In what capacity did you exist prior to registration?

The theater did not exist

3. Name the productions in your repertoire:

V. Kotenko	N. Mokroborodova	*The Iron Curtain*
A. Stavitskii	V. Shabolina	*A Reflection on 1937*
A. Masliukova	O. Ovechkin	*A Leather Coat from a Parachute Is for Sale*
E. Chepovetskii	N. Mokroborodova	*Kytsyk i Mytsyk* (Pol.)
V. Zimin	V. Zimin	*Chubrik*
Lindsberg	V. Poletaev	*The Kid and Carlson*

4. If possible, please formulate the creative credo of your studio and the principles of your association (the creative, organizational, commercial, and humane goals)

An active theater (with the participation of the audience)
Shock theater (social pressure points)
A mysterious theater (multiple levels of reality)

5. How many people are in your collective today? 8

Men: 3

Women: 5

younger than 25 years: 2

from 26 to 35: 4

from 36 to 45: 2

How many people have a theater education? 6

6. What are the average earnings of the actors in your studio?

On an average 150 rubles. (a real approximation)

7. Do you have your own rehearsal space?

c) No, we have to rehearse wherever we can

9. By what means do you prepare decorations, costumes, props, and so forth?

d) We prepare them ourselves

10. Do you have a special permanent location for the storage of your props?

b) We do not have a special location, but use the rehearsal space at other locations

c) No, the props are kept in the apartments of the studio members

11. Do you have a permanent location for the run of a production? No

17. What is the average price of a ticket to a production at your theater?

At the permanent location 1.5 rubles

On tour 1.5-2 rubles

18. What problems did you run into as your studio came into being?

The theater is not needed in Leningrad; there is no movement toward acceptance and from this comes the instability of the personnel. An absence of advertisement, critics, location, and subsidy.

19. What most of all worries you and alarms you at the present time?

The spiritual degeneration out of which flows the absence of aesthetic spiritual needs; the theater remains unwanted.

20. In your opinion, how could government and societal organizations show support for you?

The theater must be subsidized. There must be a permanent rehearsal space and a staging area with a minimal rent payment.

21. In your opinion, what is the central problem in the life of your studio?

"Knives" between the project and the incarnation, between that which is desired and that which is real.

22. In your opinion, what is the central problem in the life of contemporary Soviet theater?

The general decline of the audience's interest; the audience is not going to the theater. The former false theater has regressed with the loss of the artistic and aesthetic point of reference.

QUESTIONNAIRES

The Leningrad Student Theater
(Ленинградский студенческий театр)
4/20/90

1. When was your collective officially registered in accordance with the regulations for theater-studios?

January 1986

2. When was your first production performed?

April 1945

At which institution was your theater-studio registered?

a) The Culture Administration

d) A student club of Leningrad State University

In what capacity did you exist prior to registration?

Both before and after, as an amateur collective. Sometimes when necessary we invite professionals. For example, *Marat/Sade* by Weiss and *And a Light Shines in the Darkness* by L. Tolstoy.

3. Name the productions in your repertoire:

V. Siniakevich	Golikov	*The Beast*
M. Gindin		
L. Tolstoy	Golikov	*And a Light Shines in the Darkness*
L. Petrushevskaia	Golikov	*Bimbonada* or *Songs of the 20th Century*
In rehearsal:		
V. Aksenov	Golikov	*Surplussed Barrelware*
Planned:		
Orwell	Golikov	*Animal Farm*

4. If possible, please formulate the creative credo of your studio and the principles of your association (the creative, organizational, commercial, and humane goals)

The realization of the demand to speak about the most important things (what is sad and happy, frightening and funny) by the means of the favorite art in the company of people who are like each other.

5. How many people are in your collective today? 30

Men: 13

Women: 17

younger than 25 years: 10

from 26 to 35: 15

from 46 to 55: 5

How many people have a theater education? 3

7. Do you have your own rehearsal space?

c) No, we have to rehearse wherever we can

8. What are the dimensions of the rehearsal space which you use?

From 0 to infinity

9. By what means do you prepare decorations, costumes, props, and so forth?

e) Everything a little at a time

10. Do you have a special permanent location for the storage of your props?

a) Yes

11. Do you have a permanent location for the run of a production? No

13. What is the usual attendance? From 200 to 50

14. Was it necessary for you to re-equip this location?

b) Cosmetic work was done (from time to time)

What was accommodated at your location before it was given to the theater?

Academic classrooms

15. How many presentations did your studio give in 1989? About 20

    at other locations

    in Leningrad: about 15 productions

    on tour: about 5 productions

16. How many spectators attended productions in your studio in 1989?

Approximately 2000 spectators

Of this number 500 spectators on tour

17. What is the average price of a ticket to a production at your theater?

At the permanent location 1.5 rubles

On tour 1.5 rubles

18. What problems did you run into as your studio came into being?

1) The creative problems of each production depending on the author and genre.

2) The struggle with the dilettantism of the amateurs.

3) The endless problems with the lack of a permanent location for rehearsal and performance.

19. What most of all worries you and alarms you at the present time?

The absence of a location and in connection with this a decrease in the influx of new forces [participants] and the audience.

20. In your opinion, how could government and societal organizations show support for you?

They not only could, but are obligated to grant a permanent location, because we have provoked the interest of the public and critics for a long time.

21. In your opinion, what is the central problem in the life of your studio?

In general, dilettantism. Today, a location is more important than anything.

22. In your opinion, what is the central problem in the life of contemporary Soviet theater?

To teach itself to speak directly about the important things (of course in a figurative form) and not by hints and codes.

The City (Город)
4/17/89

1. When was your collective officially registered in accordance with the regulations for theater-studios?

November 1988

2. When was your first production performed?

May 1987

At which institution was your theater-studio registered?

b) The Youth Culture Center (Dzerzhinskii and Oktiabr'skii Districts)

In what capacity did you exist prior to registration?

In the capacity of a theater-studio, but without a roof and the possibility to perform for our own audience.

3. Name the productions in your repertoire:

Triptych based on A. Remez, V. Rasputin, V. Tokareva	S. Kurbatova	*Urban Etudes*
K. Sergienko*	S. Kurbatova	*Dogs*
R. Kipling	S. Kurbatova	*The Cat That Walked by Himself*
Farewell Ravine*		

4. If possible, please formulate the creative credo of your studio and the principles of your association (the creative, organizational, commercial, and humane goals)

Least of all, we would like to be called a theater, least of all the people who come here want to be called actors. We need to remember who we are and what we were at one time. Through the body-memory, through the whole soul, we must finally learn not to act, otherwise we all will perish.

5. How many people are in your collective today? 8

Men: 4

Women: 4

younger than 25 years: 5

from 26 to 35: 3

7. Do you have your own rehearsal space?

a) Yes, we have our own

8. What are the dimensions of the rehearsal space which you use?

100 m^2

9. By what means do you prepare decorations, costumes, props, and so forth?

d) We prepare them ourselves

10. Do you have a special permanent location for the storage of your props?

a) Yes

11. Do you have a permanent location for the run of a production? Yes

12. What is real capacity of your hall? 100

13. What is the usual attendance?

We have played for seventy and the hall was full.

14. Was it necessary for you to re-equip this location?

b) Cosmetic work was done

What was accommodated at your location before it was given to the theater?

A video salon of the October District

17. What is the average price of a ticket to a production at your theater?

At the permanent location 1.4 rubles

On tour 2 rubles

18. What problems did you run into as your studio came into being?

The human [problems]. Not everyone has the strength to endure, not every one wants to dig into one's personal feelings. More often, problems in living attract a person, to enjoy oneself, to make friends, to sleep with someone. We are in search of those who have not yet died.

19. What most of all worries you and alarms you at the present time?

My people, each of whom is unique, are impossible to replace. And everything is shaky. And life is a complicated thing, but this does not reassure [one]. One simply wants a production to live and that we might be together. Always or as long as possible.

20. In your opinion, how could government and societal organizations show support for you?

The October SPMTS (Sovmestnoe predpriiatie molodezhnogo tsentra) Joint Enterprise is a remarkable organization which always helps us and everyone. And it is never necessary to prove anything to anyone. This is fantastic. What people!

21. In your opinion, what is the central problem in the life of your studio?

To learn not to lie. In life and in mutual relations. Sometimes this is dangerous for [your] life. But that work which we are doing demands colossal human efforts. Otherwise it is not worth it. It is funny when you are thirty to be involved in amateur work.

22. In your opinion, what is the central problem in the life of contemporary Soviet theater?

The very same. People have forgotten how to speak about what troubles them. The theater has turned into a low farce with fools. All cry, though it is not sad. In the theater people are searching for what is real. They do not find it and go away. Right now, practically no one is going to the theater, have you noticed this?

I and Thou (Я и ты)
4/10/90

1. When was your collective officially registered in accordance with the regulations for theater-studios?

September 1988

2. When was your first production performed?

March 1989

At which institution was your theater-studio registered?

b) The Youth Culture Center (Kuibyshevskii District)

In what capacity did you exist prior to registration?

An amateur theater-studio

3. Name the productions in your repertoire:

A. Sokolova	Alla A. Reznikova	*People, Beasts, and Bananas*
L. Petrushevskaia	Alla A. Reznikova	*Andante*

4. If possible, please formulate the creative credo of your studio and the principles of your association (the creative, organizational, commercial, and humane goals)

A theater community

5. How many people are in your collective today? 13

Men: 5

Women: 8

younger than 25 years: 13

7. Do you have your own rehearsal space?

a) Yes, we have our own

8. What are the dimensions of the rehearsal space which you use?

100 m^2

9. By what means do you prepare decorations, costumes, props, and so forth?

QUESTIONNAIRES

d) We prepare them ourselves

10. Do you have a special permanent location for the storage of your props?

a) Yes

11. Do you have a permanent location for the run of a production? Yes

12. What is real capacity of your hall? 50

13. What is the usual attendance? 40

14. Was it necessary for you to re-equip this location?

b) Cosmetic work was done

What was accommodated at your location before it was given to the theater?

A Comrades Court of the Housing Office

15. How many presentations did your studio give in 1989? 4 productions

       at your own location: 3 productions

       at other locations

       on tour: 1 production

16. How many spectators attended productions in your studio in 1989?

Approximately 150 spectators

Of this number 50 spectators on tour

18. What problems did you run into as your studio came into being?

They took away our locations

19. What most of all worries you and alarms you at the present time?

How to build further work in the studio in order to move on to a different level

20. In your opinion, how could government and societal organizations show support for you?

By not taking away our location

21. In your opinion, what is the central problem in the life of your studio?

Human relations and creative growth

22. In your opinion, what is the central problem in the life of contemporary Soviet theater?

The lack of a global sensibility

Your address: Kolokol'naia, dom 5
Telephone: 113-32-25

QUESTIONNAIRES

The Comedians (Комедианты)
3/16/90

1. When was your collective officially registered in accordance with the regulations for theater-studios?

September 1988

2. When was your first production performed?

June 1988

At which institution was your theater-studio registered?

b) The Youth Culture Center Lenin District

In what capacity did you exist prior to registration?

A group of artists-professionals having done a performance and running it from the Youth Culture Center of the Lenin District

3. Name the productions in your repertoire:

A composition based on the works by E. de Filippo (the plays: *The Cylinder, Risk, Photo for Mommy*); author of the composition, M. Levshin; author of the song texts, Iu. Borisov	M. A. Levshin	*Passions Italian Style*
G. Saphir and Prokof'ev	Levshin	*Puss-in-Boots*

4. If possible, please formulate the creative credo of your studio and the principles of your association (the creative, organizational, commercial, and humane goals)

The rebirth of the comic genre. Classic and contemporary comedy from Moli`ere on, the actor, the mastery (the rebirth) of their goals and the genre. Comedy rich in content and humane, not void of poetry and civic spirit.

5. How many people are in your collective today? 10

Men: 7

Women: 3

younger than 25 years: 1

from 26 to 35: 5

from 36 to 45: 3

from 46 to 55: 1

How many people have a theater education? 10

6. What are the average earnings of the actors in your studio?

On an average 150 rubles.

7. Do you have your own rehearsal space?

c) No, we have to rehearse wherever we can

8. What are the dimensions of the rehearsal space which you use?

100 m^2 (small hall)

9. By what means do you prepare decorations, costumes, props, and so forth?

d) We prepare them ourselves

10. Do you have a special permanent location for the storage of your props?

b) We do not have a special location, but use the rehearsal space or other locations

11. Do you have a permanent location for the run of a production? No

What was accommodated at your location before it was given to the theater?

To rehearse, store props

15. How many presentations did your studio give in 1989? 71 productions

      at other locations

      in Leningrad: 71 productions

      on tour: 42 productions

16. How many spectators attended productions in your studio in 1989?

Approximately 21,000 spectators

QUESTIONNAIRES

Of this number 15,000 spectators on tour

17. What is the average price of a ticket to a production at your theater?

At the permanent location 1.5 rubles

On tour 2 rubles

18. What problems did you run into as your studio came into being?

The problem of creative and human compatibility. The problem of the endlessly long acquisition of the status of the State theater at the Leningrad District Culture Administration

19. What most of all worries you and alarms you at the present time?

A location

20. In your opinion, how could government and societal organizations show support for you?

A location, the illumination of the theater activity by means of mass information

21. In your opinion, what is the central problem in the life of your studio?

The education of professionally equipped artists and not an invitation to those who are already "prepared"

22. In your opinion, what is the central problem in the life of contemporary Soviet theater?

The lack of a genuine respect for theater art (on all levels)

QUESTIONNAIRES

The Puppet (Кукла)
4/6/90

1. When was your collective officially registered in accordance with the regulations for theater-studios?

June 1988

2. When was your first production performed?

May 1987

At which institution was your theater-studio registered?

a) The Culture Administration

In what capacity did you exist prior to registration?

A theater

3. Name the productions in your repertoire:

M. de Gelderodes	E. Ugriumov	*The Pathetic Death of an Actor*
M. de Gelderodes	E. Ugriumov	*Escorial*
A. P. Chekhov	E. Ugriumov	*All Must Be Beautiful in a Person*
B. Shergin (adapt. by director)	E. Ugriumov	*The Magic Ring*
B. Gauff (adapt. by director)	E. Ugriumov	*Dwarf Nose*
D. Urban	I. Myshkin	*All Mice Love Cheese*
H. C. Andersen	E. Ugriumov	*Andersen's Fairy Tales*
E. Ugriumov	E. Ugriumov	*How the Crocodile and the Hare Lived Happily Ever After*
Jack London (adapt. by director)	I. Myshkin	*The Legend of the Shaman*

4. If possible, please formulate the creative credo of your studio and the principles of your association (the creative, organizational, commercial, and humane goals)

Creative-the creation of plays
Organizational-financial--the creation of a collective capable of surviving and living independently
Humane-a collective created on the basis of love for each other

5. How many people are in your collective today? 20

Men: 10

Women: 10

younger than 25 years: 9

from 26 to 35: 6

from 36 to 45: 5

How many people have a theater education? 10

6. What are the average earnings of the actors in your studio?

On an average 180 rubles.

7. Do you have your own rehearsal space?

c) No, we have to rehearse wherever we can

9. By what means do you prepare decorations, costumes, props, and so forth?

d) We prepare them ourselves

10. Do you have a special permanent location for the storage of your props?

b) We do not have a special location, but use the rehearsal space or other locations

11. Do you have a permanent location for the run of a production? No

14. Was it necessary for you to re-equip this location?

a) No, no work was done

15. How many presentations did your studio give in 1989? 240 productions

      at other locations

      on tour: 80 productions

16. How many spectators attended productions in your studio in 1989?

Approximately 50,000 spectators

Of this number 18,000 spectators on tour

17. What is the average price of a ticket to a production at your theater?

At the permanent location 1.20 rubles

On tour 1.50 rubles

18. What problems did you run into as your studio came into being?

The problem of a location
The selection of an administration
The shortage of the means for existence

19. What most of all worries you and alarms you at the present time?

The problem of a location

20. In your opinion, how could government and societal organizations show support for you?

To allot a location

21. In your opinion, what is the central problem in the life of your studio?

location

22. In your opinion, what is the central problem in the life of contemporary Soviet theater?

The low level of culture

QUESTIONNAIRES

The Mummers (Лицедеи)*

1. When was your collective officially registered in accordance with the regulations for theater-studios?

1988

2. When was your first production performed?

1968

At which institution was your theater-studio registered?

a) The Culture Administration

In what capacity did you exist prior to registration?

1967 studio; 1978 creative studio; 1979 ensemble; 1980 theater-studio; 1986 clown-mime theater; 1988 theater-studio

3. Name the productions in your repertoire:

Polunin, Skvortsov, Rozinskii	Rozinskii	*Twenty-one Novellas*
A. Belinskii	Belinskii	*Love the Pedestrian*
Polunin, Skvortsov, Makeev	Polunin	*Mime Improvisation*
Polunin, Skvortsov	Polunin	*Visionaries*
Polunin, Skvortsov	Polunin, Gertsman	*Actors*
Musorgskii (Polunin)	Polunin	*Pictures from a Show*
Polunin	Polunin	*Attics*
Polunin	Polunin, Dmitrienko	*The Brave Boy*
Kislev, Polunin	Kislev, Polunin	*Petrushka*
Polunin	Polunin	*The Catastrophe*
Polunin	Polunin	*The Wedding*
Polunin	Polunin	*Dreams*

4. If possible, please formulate the creative credo of your studio and the principles of your association (the creative, organizational, commercial, and humane goals)

The goals for the rebirth of the folk theater, pantomime, clownery, street theater, burlesque, film, and carnivals

5. How many people are in your collective today? 20

Men: 15

Woemn: 5

from 36 to 45: 12

from 46 to 55: 4

older than 56: 4

6. What are the average earnings of the actors in your studio?

An average of 500 rubles.

7. Do you have your own rehearsal space?

a) Yes, we have our own

8. What are the dimensions of the rehearsal space which you use?

100 m^2

9. By what means do you prepare decorations, costumes, props, and so forth?

b) We use what we have

c) We rent

d) We prepare them ourselves (basically)

10. Do you have a special permanent location for the storage of your props?

a) Yes

11. Do you have a permanent location for the run of a production?

No and it is not needed

12. What is real capacity of your hall? From 10 to 10,000

13. What is the usual attendance? Packed

14. Was it necessary for you to re-equip this location?

c) We essentially had to re-equip the location

15. How many presentations did your studio give in 1989? 250 productions

at other locations

in Leningrad: 20 productions

16. How many spectators attended productions in your studio in 1989?

Approximately 37,500 spectators

17. What is the average price of a ticket to a production at your theater?

At the permanent location 4 rubles

On tour 5 rubles ($20-30)

18. What problems did you run into as your studio came into being?

With all kinds (no professional administrators) and nothing on sale to equip a production

19. What most of all worries you and alarms you at the present time?

To have the free time for creativity and to create an international center in Leningrad, perhaps a building.

20. In your opinion, how could government and societal organizations show support for you?

Necessary land or an old building

Your address: 197022 Leningrad, Nab. reki Karpovki, d. 45ª
Telephone: 234-58-19

*Litsedei is an archaic and comical word which essentially means actor. Though "riazhenye" is traditionally translated as mummers (note their appearance in Chekhov's *The Cherry Orchard*), it is felt that this translation would also be appropriate here. "Expressionists" and "impressionists" seem not to convey the feeling that these are essentially proletarian players who are adept, based on the root of the Russian word, at making faces. See *Slovar' sovremennogo russkogo literaturnogo iazyka*, tom 6 (Moskva: Akademiia Nauk SSSR, 1957), p. 283.

QUESTIONNAIRES

The Leningrad State Theater-Studio
(Ленинградский государственный театр-студия)
Directed by Larisa Malevannaia

1. When was your collective officially registered in accordance with the regulations for theater-studios?

September 1988

2. When was your first production performed?

December 1988

At which institution was your theater-studio registered?

a) The Culture Administration

In what capacity did you exist prior to registration?

As a graduate course of the Leningrad State Theater Institute

3. Name the productions in your repertoire:

O. Ernov	O. Pal'mov	*We Arrived*
V. Malkov (also dir.)	O. Pal'mov	*Christmas*
O. Pal'mov, L. Malevannaia	L. Malevannaia, O. Pal'mov	*Theater, Theater, Theater*
N. Sadur	Kaminskii	*Loving People*
M. Mokienko	M. Mokienko	*The New Year Adventures of a Computer Virus*

4. If possible, please formulate the creative credo of your studio and the principles of your association (the creative, organizational, commercial, and humane goals)

Yet another attempt despite society and the times to create a living theater, to create a unity from various individualities. To teach young actors the conscious direction of personal energy.

5. How many people are in your collective today? 30

Men: 20

Women: 10

younger than 25 years: 3

from 26 to 35: 17

from 36 to 45: 7

from 46 to 55: 3

6. What are the average earnings of the actors in your studio?

An average of 135 rubles.

7. Do you have your own rehearsal space?

c) No, we have to rehearse wherever we can

9. By what means do you prepare decorations, costumes, props, and so forth?

d) We prepare them ourselves

e) We order them from other theaters and cooperatives

10. Do you have a special permanent location for the storage of your props?

b) We do not have a special location, but use the rehearsal space or other locations

c) No, the props are kept in the apartments of the studio members

11. Do you have a permanent location for the run of a production?

No, but now the location of the former Iakovlev club is being reconditioned.

14. Was it necessary for you to re-equip this location?

c) We essentially had to re-equip the location

What was accommodated at your location before it was given to the theater?

The location was not used for two years since it was destroyed after a fire.

15. How many presentations did your studio give in 1989? 65 productions

        at other locations

        in Leningrad: 55 productions

        on tour: 10 productions

16. How many spectators attended productions in your studio in 1989?

Approximately 19,500 spectators

Of this number 3,000 spectators on tour

17. What is the average price of a ticket to a production at your theater?

At the permanent location 2 rubles

On tour 3 rubles

18. What problems did you run into as your studio came into being?

The lack of a demand for the art of the theater by the public and by the representatives of State organizations.

19. What most of all worries you and alarms you at the present time?

That the period mentioned above will continue.

20. In your opinion, how could government and societal organizations show support for you?

By fulfilling the earlier promises regarding the repair of the building and accordingly by making it ready for use.
In the organization of advertising.

21. In your opinion, what is the central problem in the life of your studio?

Homelessness

22. In your opinion, what is the central problem in the life of contemporary Soviet theater?

The public does not need the theater right now. Whoever has the possibility and strength not to fuss is winning.

QUESTIONNAIRES 135

The Mimegrants (Мимигранты)
2/16/90

1. When was your collective officially registered in accordance with the regulations for theater-studios?

May 1989

2. When was your first production performed?

September 1989

At which institution was your theater-studio registered?

d) The Youth Center Otava (Aftermath) with the Komsomol Committee at the Kirov Factory.

In what capacity did you exist prior to registration?

A pantomime studio at the Palace of Culture

3. Name the productions in your repertoire:

A. N. Pliushch   A. N. Pliushch   *The Comedy with a Murder*

4. If possible, please formulate the creative credo of your studio and the principles of your association (the creative, organizational, commercial, and humane goals)

To be necessary to the spectator, an association on purely human principles

5. How many people are in your collective today? 5

Men: 5

younger than 25 years: 4

from 26 to 35: 1

6. What are the average earnings of the actors in your studio?

An average of 150 rubles.

7. Do you have your own rehearsal space?

c) No, we have to rehearse wherever we can

8. What are the dimensions of the rehearsal space which you use?

20 m²

9. By what means do you prepare decorations, costumes, props, and so forth?

d) We prepare them ourselves

10. Do you have a special permanent location for the storage of your props?

a) Yes

11. Do you have a permanent location for the run of a production? No

15. How many presentations did your studio give in 1989? 20-25

> at other locations
>
> in Leningrad: 15-20 productions
>
> on tour: 10 productions

16. How many spectators attended productions in your studio in 1989?

Approximately 500-1500 spectators

Of this number 1000 spectators on tour

17. What is the average price of a ticket to a production at your theater?

On tour 2-2.5 rubles

18. What problems did you run into as your studio came into being?

a) Our own location

b) There was no place for our production

19. What most of all worries you and alarms you at the present time?

The possibility to prepare a new production

20. In your opinion, how could government and societal organizations show support for you?

There is nowhere to show our productions

21. In your opinion, what is the central problem in the life of your studio?

The impossibility to decide creative questions due to financial difficulties.

22. In your opinion, what is the central problem in the life of contemporary Soviet theater?

Artistic truth

QUESTIONNAIRES

The Mime Theater "Jester" (Мим-театр «Шут»)
4/12/90

1. When was your collective officially registered in accordance with the regulations for theater-studios?

August 1989

2. When was your first production performed?

December 1987

At which institution was your theater-studio registered?

b) The Youth Culture Center (Vyborgskii District, Leningrad)

d) Leningrad's Creative Association "Comrade" at the Krasnosel'skii Raiispolkom

In what capacity did you exist prior to registration?

As a pantomime studio in an institute of higher education

3. Name the productions in your repertoire:

A. Bachmanov	A. Bachmanov	*Mimemix*
A. Bachmanov	A. Bachmanov	*Masquerade*

Also a number of street performances which are created and performed each time in a new way, depending on the situation and environment.

4. If possible, please formulate the creative credo of your studio and the principles of your association (the creative, organizational, commercial, and humane goals)

The creative principles are formulated in the name of the collective: the clown (fool), as an actor and personality, is intellectually and emotionally developed, prepared for improvisation.

Organizational-commercial: payment depends on the quantity and quality of the invested work. An organizational democracy and creative dictatorship. The basic bond of the collective is the personal affection towards each other.

5. How many people are in your collective today? 6

Men: 4

Women: 2

younger than 25 years: 4

from 26 to 35: 2

6. What are the average earnings of the actors in your studio?

An average of 50 rubles.

7. Do you have your own rehearsal location?

d) We rehearse at the location of the pantomime studio at the Ordzhonikidze Palace of Culture

8. What are the dimensions of the rehearsal space which you use?

100 m^2

9. By what means do you prepare decorations, costumes, props, and so forth?

b) We use what we have

d) We prepare them ourselves

10. Do you have a special permanent location for the storage of your props?

c) No, the props are kept in the apartments of the studio members

11. Do you have a permanent location for the run of a production? No

15. How many presentations did your studio give in 1989? About 60

        in Leningrad: about 60 productions

16. How many spectators attended productions in your studio in 1989?

Approximately 6000 spectators

17. What is the average price of a ticket to a production at your theater?

We work on the basis of a guarantee.

18. What problems did you run into as your studio came into being?

Basically the problem of creating the collective.

19. What most of all worries you and alarms you at the present time?

The raising of the creative level of actors, the search for new theater forms, [and] the stability of the collective membership

20. In your opinion, how could government and societal organizations show support for you?

By providing a location for rehearsals and performances; management

21. In your opinion, what is the central problem in the life of your studio?

The amateur status of the actors inhibits the concentration in their lives on the theater.

22. In your opinion, what is the central problem in the life of contemporary Soviet theater?

The monotony of theatrical forms connected with the monotony of theater schools.

The Young Theater (Молодой театр)

1. When was your collective officially registered in accordance with the regulations for theater-studios?

June 1988

2. When was your first production performed?

May 1988

At which institution was your theater-studio registered?

a) The Culture Administration

In what capacity did you exist prior to registration?

In the capacity of a touring theater at the Leningrad Association "Lenconcert"

3. Name the productions in your repertoire:

Viktor Rozov	Spivak	*The Blow*
Liudmila Razumovskaia	Spivak	*Dear Elena Sergeevna*
Slawomir Mrozek	Spivak	*Tango*

4. If possible, please formulate the creative credo of your studio and the principles of your association (the creative, organizational, commercial, and humane goals)

Back to Stanislavsky

5. How many people are in your collective today? 17

Men: 10

Women: 7

How many people have a theater education? 17

6. What are the average earnings of the actors in your studio?

An average of 150 rubles.

7. Do you have your own permanent location?

a) Yes, we have our own

8. What are the dimensions of the rehearsal space which you use?

35 m²

9. By what means do you prepare decorations, costumes, props, and so forth?

a) We order them from an artistic staging complex

10. Do you have a special permanent location for the storage of your props?

a) Yes

11. Do you have a permanent location for the run of a production? Yes

12. What is the real capacity of your hall? 225

13. What is the usual attendance? 85%

14. Was it necessary for you to re-equip this location?

a) No, no work was done

What was accommodated at your location before it was given to the theater?

The district theater Vremia

17. What is the average price of a ticket to a production at your theater?

At the permanent location 3 rubles

18. What problems did you run into as your studio came into being?

The theater's location must be its own. Normal subsidies calculated and paid.

20. In your opinion, how could government and societal organizations show support for you?

Financial help

21. In your opinion, what is the central problem in the life of your studio?

Financially!!!

22. In your opinion, what is the central problem in the life of contemporary Soviet theater?

Financially!!!

The Bridge (MOCT)
2/15/90

1. When was your collective officially registered in accordance with the regulations for theater-studios?

July 1988

2. When was your first production performed?

September 1988

At which institution was your theater-studio registered?

a) The Culture Administration

In what capacity did you exist prior to registration?

Did not exist.

3. Name the productions in your repertoire:

V. Billevich, L. Iakubovich	V. Iavich	*The Hotel with Ghosts*
V. Iavich	V. Iavich	*The War with the Magopachi*
Kotenko	V. Iavich	*The Iron Curtain*

4. If possible, please formulate the creative credo of your studio and the principles of your association (the creative, organizational, commercial, and humane goals)

Opposition to official art

5. How many people are in your collective today? 12

Men: 7

Women: 5

younger than 25 years: 3

from 26 to 35: 6

from 36 to 45: 3

How many people have a theater education? Everyone

6. What are the average earnings of the actors in your studio?

An average of 200 rubles.

7. Do you have your own permanent location?

b) No, we rent a permanent location

8. What are the dimensions of the rehearsal space which you use?

60 m^2

9. By what means do you prepare decorations, costumes, props, and so forth?

e) Underground

10. Do you have a special permanent location for the storage of your props?

b) We do not have a special location, but use the rehearsal space or other locations

11. Do you have a permanent location for the run of a production? No

15. How many presentations did your studio give in 1989?

    In half a year: 60 productions

    at your own location: 3 productions

    at other locations

    in Leningrad: 3 productions

    on tour: 57 productions

16. How many spectators attended productions in your studio in 1989?

Approximately 3000 spectators

Of this number 2800 spectators on tour

17. What is the average price of a ticket to a production at your theater?

At the permanent location 2 rubles

On tour 3 rubles

18. What problems did you run into as your studio came into being?

a) The lack of a base
b) The lack of finances

c) The lack of a common school (of theater training)
d) The lack of a general goal

19. What most of all worries you and alarms you at the present time?

The family

20. In your opinion, how could government and societal organizations show support for you?

In no way today, since in June of last year (1989), I parted with the studio. Now it is called Nevsky prospekt. Incidentally, I came up with the name.

21. In your opinion, what is the central problem in the life of your studio?

In principle, nothing.

22. In your opinion, what is the central problem in the life of contemporary Soviet theater?

As it is throughout the entire country, totalitarian feudalism.

QUESTIONNAIRES

The Theater-Studio on Lesnoi (Театр-студия на Лесном)
3/11/90

1. When was your collective officially registered in accordance with the regulations for theater-studios?

1977

2. When was your first production performed?

March 1974

At which institution was your theater-studio registered?

a) The Culture Administration

In what capacity did you exist prior to registration?

A student theater at the Leningradskii Politekhnicheskii Institut im. Kalinina

3. Name the productions in your repertoire:

K. Khoinskii	V. Suslov	*Night Tale*
V. Tendriakov	V. Suslov	*The Night After Graduation*
V. Suslov	V. Suslov	*The Lay of Igor's Campaign*
Vs. Vishnevskii	V. Suslov	*The Optimistic Tragedy*
A. Blok	V. Suslov	*The Rose and the Cross*
E. Nosov	V. Suslov	*Usviatski Helmet Bearers*
E. Shvarts	V. Suslov	*The Dragon*
G. Baklanov	V. Suslov	*Friends*
N. Matukovskii	V. Suslov	*The Measurer of Wisdom*
M. Shatrov	V. Suslov	*Dictatorship of Conscience*
E. Radzinskii	V. Suslov	*Theater in the Days of Nero and Seneca*
L. Andreev	V. Suslov	*Judas Iscariot*
K. Simonov	V. Suslov	*The Fourth*

4. If possible, please formulate the creative credo of your studio and the principles of your association (the creative, organizational, commercial, and humane goals)

A love for the theater

5. How many people are in your collective today? 13

Men: 9

Women: 4

younger than 25 years: 3

from 26 to 35: 8

from 36 to 45: 2

How many people have a theater education? 2

6. What are the average earnings of the actors in your studio?

An average of 0 rubles.

7. Do you have your own rehearsal location?

a) Yes, we have our own

8. What are the dimensions of the rehearsal space which you use?

160 m^2

9. By what means do you prepare decorations, costumes, props, and so forth?

d) We prepare them ourselves

10. Do you have a special permanent location for the storage of your props?

a) Yes

11. Do you have a permanent location for the run of a production? Yes

12. What is real capacity of your hall? 100

13. What is the usual attendance? 80-100

14. Was it necessary for you to re-equip this location?

c) We essentially had to re-equip the location

What was accommodated at your location before it was given to the theater?

A dance class

15. How many presentations did your studio give in 1989? 16

       at your own location: 14 productions

       at other locations

       on tour: 2 productions

16. How many spectators attended productions in your studio in 1989?

Approximately 1800 spectators

Of this number 300 spectators on tour

17. What is the average price of a ticket to a production at your theater?

At the permanent location 1.5 rubles

On tour 1.5 rubles

18. What problems did you run into as your studio came into being?

Pressure from the Party organizations at the Institute

19. What most of all worries you and alarms you at the present time?

A lack of time for carrying out rehearsals and performances.

20. In your opinion, how could government and societal organizations show support for you?

Financial support

21. In your opinion, what is the central problem in the life of your studio?

A decline in the audience's interest

22. In your opinion, what is the central problem in the life of contemporary Soviet theater?

A decline in the audience's interest

Your address: Leningrad, pr. Lesnoi, d. 65
Telephone: 245-37-61

The House of the People (Народный дом)*
2/10/90

1. When was your collective officially registered in accordance with the regulations for theater-studios?

June 10, 1988

2. When was your first production performed?

September 20, 1988

At which institution was your theater-studio registered?

a) The Culture Administration

In what capacity did you exist prior to registration?

We did not exist.

3. Name the productions in your repertoire:

V. Nabokov	L. Rakhlin	*The Event*
M. Varfolomeev	L. Rakhlin	*The Period of Residence Is Over*
T. Arkhangel'skaia, I. Rogachii, B. Vishnevskii, M. Pashkov	(Authors)	*We Play the King*
J. Anouilh	L. Rakhlin	*Generals in Skirts*
T. Arkhangel'skaia, I. Kovalenko, M. Pashkov	E. Ryzhik	*If You Skin a Cat, Then It Is the Spitting Image of a Rabbit*

4. If possible, please formulate the creative credo of your studio and the principles of your association (the creative, organizational, commercial, and humane goals)

5. How many people are in your collective today? 11

Men: 6

Women: 5

younger than 25 years: 2

from 26 to 35: 6

from 36 to 45: 2

from 46 to 55: 1

How many people have a theater education? 11

6. What are the average earnings of the actors in your studio?

On an average 140 rubles.

7. Do you have your own permanent location?

a) Yes, we have our own (until February 1, 1990)

9. By what means do you prepare decorations, costumes, props, and so forth?

b) We use what we have

d) We prepare them ourselves

10. Do you have a special permanent location for the storage of your props?

a) Yes (until February 1, 1990)

11. Do you have a permanent location for the run of a production?

Yes (until February 1, 1990)

12. What is real capacity of your hall? 300

13. What is the usual attendance? 200

14. Was it necessary for you to re-equip this location?

a) No, no work was done

What was accommodated at your location before it was given to the theater?

It was a movie house.

15. How many presentations did your studio give in 1989? About 300

  at your own location: about 270 productions

  at other locations

  on tour: about 30 productions

16. How many spectators attended productions in your studio in 1989?

Approximately 60,000 spectators

Of this number 10,000 spectators on tour

17. What is the average price of a ticket to a production at your theater?

At the permanent location 2.40 rubles

On tour 2.5 rubles

18. What problems did you run into as your studio came into being?

The problem in the selection of the repertoire.

19. What most of all worries you and alarms you at the present time?

The absence of an interest among officials of various ranks and the bureaucrats of culture in the work of the theater-studios and in the development of the theater in general. There is a crisis in the theater, and Narodnyi dom is in that number.

20. In your opinion, how could government and societal organizations show support for you?

In the acquisition of a location, in the organization of the normal life of theater (money, money, money), in the organization of advertising.

21. In your opinion, what is the central problem in the life of your studio?

The absence of a proper location and continuous financial difficulties.

22. In your opinion, what is the central problem in the life of contemporary Soviet theater?

The terrible, inhuman conditions, in which the country's theaters have been placed. The loss in the culture of theater attendance. The general decline of culture. The attempts to direct culture from above.

*The word дом in Russian has a variety of meanings. For example, it can refer to a large apartment building. In this context, the title may convey the idea of a civic center.

QUESTIONNAIRES

Four Little Windows (Четыре окошка)
2/10/90

1. When was your collective officially registered in accordance with the regulations for theater-studios?

It is not registered.

2. When was your first production performed?

January 1978

At which institution was your theater-studio registered?

The V. I. Lenin Palace of Culture as a production association at the "Bolshevik Factory."

In what capacity did you exist prior to registration?

The dramatic collective at the club of the factory "Bolshevik" existed for a long time; it received the name of "people's" in the sixties, but in its present form and under the name Four Little Windows, it has existed for twelve years.

3. Name the productions in your repertoire:

1978 M. Kulish	L. Shvarts, T. Zhakovskaia	*Thus Perished Guska*
1979 A. Volodin	T. Zhakovskaia	*Sister Hope*
1980 E. Shvarts	T. Zhakovskaia	*The Dragon*
1981 S. Zlotnikov	T. Zhakovskaia	*A Man Came to a Woman*
1982 S. Zlotnikov	L. Shvarts	*The Command*
1983 B. Vasil'ev	T. Zhakovskaia	*My Horses are Flying*
1987 W. Shakespeare	T. Zhakovskaia	*We Act Hamlet*
1988 E. Shvarts	T. Zhakovskaia	*The Dragon* (2nd editing)
1989 T. Williams	T. Zhakovskaia	*The Night of the Iguana*
1989 D. Kharms	O. Tsekhnovitser	*Kharms for an Hour*
1990 S. Zlotnikov	V. Kuteinikov	*Scenes by the Fountain*

4. If possible, please formulate the creative credo of your studio and the principles of your association (the creative, organizational, commercial, and humane goals)

It is a club of self-education, theater therapy, a refuge, a reserve of mutants (social anomalies), a house, an insane asylum, all this or at the same time.

5. How many people are in your collective today? 30

Men: 14

Women: 16

younger than 25 years: 11

from 26 to 35: 12

from 36 to 45: 3

from 46 to 55: 4

How many people have a theater education? None

7. Do you have your own rehearsal space?

a) Yes, we have our own

8. What are the dimensions of the rehearsal space which you use?

72 m^2

9. By what means do you prepare decorations, costumes, props, and so forth?

d) We prepare them ourselves

10. Do you have a special permanent location for the storage of your props?

a) Yes

11. Do you have a permanent location for the run of a production? Yes

12. What is real capacity of your hall? 70

13. What is the usual attendance? 30-50 (from 10 to 120)

14. Was it necessary for you to re-equip this location?

c) We essentially had to re-equip the location

What was accommodated at your location before it was given to the theater?

It was a lecture hall.

15. How many presentations did your studio give in 1989? 30

       at your own location: 30 productions

16. How many spectators attended productions in your studio in 1989?

Approximately 1500 spectators

17. What is the average price of a ticket to a production at your theater?

At the permanent location 1 ruble

18. What problems did you run into as your studio came into being?

19. What most of all worries you and alarms you at the present time?

The prospect of a transition to financial self-support.

20. In your opinion, how could government and societal organizations show support for you?

To continue to pay the teachers' salaries.

21. In your opinion, what is the central problem in the life of your studio?

The prospect of financial self-support.

22. In your opinion, what is the central problem in the life of contemporary Soviet theater?

The burdensome inherited sicknesses--the isolation from world culture, from its own roots, being accustomed to single-mindedness, the incompetence of its leaders, + financial self-support.

The theater's address: Leningrad, pr. Obukhovskoi oborony, 223 DK im. Lenina

The Theater of One Actor (Театр одного актера)

1. When was your collective officially registered in accordance with the regulations for theater-studios?

January 1989

2. When was your first production performed?

February 1989

At which institution was your theater-studio registered?

d) VOTM

In what capacity did you exist prior to registration?

In the capacity of free artists.

3. Name the productions in your repertoire:

| N. V. Gogol | V. Shabalina | *The Dumb Show* |
| Alla Sokolova | V. Shabalina | *The Devil of Happiness* |

4. If possible, please formulate the creative credo of your studio and the principles of your association (the creative, organizational, commercial, and humane goals)

We are trying to return to the improvisational essence of the theater when the word and action are born simultaneously. We are attempting to find a new quality of rehearsals and the opening and existence of a production.

5. How many people are in your collective today? 2

Men: 1

Women: 1

from 36 to 45: 2

How many people have a theater education? 2

7. Do you have your own rehearsal space?

c) No, we have to rehearse wherever we can

9. By what means do you prepare decorations, costumes, props, and so forth?

b) We use what we have

10. Do you have a special permanent location for the storage of your props?

c) No, the props are kept in the apartments of the studio members

11. Do you have a permanent location for the run of a production? No

15. How many presentations did your studio give in 1989? 5

> at other locations
>
> in Leningrad: 5 productions

16. How many spectators attended productions in your studio in 1989?

Approximately 384 spectators

17. What is the average price of a ticket to a production at your theater?

At the permanent location 2 rubles

18. What problems did you run into as your studio came into being?

The fundamental problem is inside our very selves and it is impossible, and indeed, unnecessary to work on it from the outside.

19. What most of all worries you and alarms you at the present time?

Work on a new production.

20. In your opinion, how could government and societal organizations show support for you?

It would be nice to have a versatile and mobile producer. It's necessary to recreate the institution of patronage.

21. In your opinion, what is the central problem in the life of your studio?

One's own readiness to work.

The Theater-Studio of Pantomime (Театр-студия пантомима)

1. When was your collective officially registered in accordance with the regulations for theater-studios?

January 1988

2. When was your first production performed?

March 1988

At which institution was your theater-studio registered?

b) The Youth Culture Center (Vyborgskii District)

In what capacity did you exist prior to registration?

Three independent studios

3. Name the productions in your repertoire:

(Directors)

P. G. Efimov	*Variety Programs from Real Life Scenes,*
A. Bachmanov	*Genre Sketches, Satirical Miniatures, and*
A. Shedler	*Musical Parodies*
V. V. Glazkov	

4. If possible, please formulate the creative credo of your studio and the principles of your association (the creative, organizational, commercial, and humane goals)

The free expression of thoughts in the genre of pantomime and clownery

5. How many people are in your collective today? 30

Men: 18 (In the beginning of the activity; does not apply to today)

Women: 12

younger than 25 years: 26

from 26 to 35: 4

How many people have a theater education? 5

6. What are the average earnings of the actors in your studio?

On an average 12 rubles.

7. Do you have your own rehearsal space?

a) Yes, we have our own in an academic institution

8. What are the dimensions of the rehearsal space which you use?

30 m^2

9. By what means do you prepare decorations, costumes, props, and so forth?

b) We use what we have

10. Do you have a special permanent location for the storage of your props?

b) We do not have a special location, but use the rehearsal space or other locations

c) No, the props are kept in the apartments of the studio members

11. Do you have a permanent location for the run of a production? No

15. How many presentations did your studio give in 1989? 12 productions

        in Leningrad: 12 productions

16. How many spectators attended productions in your studio in 1989?

Approximately 1000 spectators

17. What is the average price of a ticket to a production at your theater?

Work by contract

18. What problems did you run into as your studio came into being?

1. The constant rise in taxes.
2. The decrease of offers.

19. What most of all worries you and alarms you at the present time?

The political situation
The economy

20. In your opinion, how could government and societal organizations show support for you?

An invitation to perform at enterprises and organizations

21. In your opinion, what is the central problem in the life of your studio?

The lack of a continual demand for a production

22. In your opinion, what is the central problem in the life of contemporary Soviet theater?

The lowering of the general level of culture.

QUESTIONNAIRES

The Comedian's Refuge (Приют комедианта)
3/7/90

1. When was your collective officially registered in accordance with the regulations for theater-studios?

December 1987

2. When was your first production performed?

January 1988

At which institution was your theater-studio registered?

c) The Regional Committee of the All-Union Leninist Communist Youth Union--the Oktiabr'skii District

3. Name the productions in your repertoire:

Iu. Tomoshevskii	V. Shabalina	*Brilliant St. Petersburg*
D. Kharms	I. Bocharova	*The Old Woman*
P. Mérimée, adapt. N. Dmitrieva	I. Kuvshinov	*Carmen, Whom You Know*
I. Brodsky, adapt. A. Kovalenko	Tomoshevskii	*The Procession*
A. Averchenko, adapt. Iu. Tomoshevskii	V. Shabalina	*The Incurable*
Iu. Tomoshevskii	D. Tytiuk	*Start to Bark Stray Dog!*
G. Garcia Marquéz, adapt. G. Tskhvirava	G. Tskhvirava	*Nobody Writes the Colonel*
A. Vvedenskii, adapt. Iu. Tomoshevskii	Tomoshevskii	*A Light Shock for the Refined Public*
	Tomoshevskii	*The Ivanov's Christmas Tree*

4. If possible, please formulate the creative credo of your studio and the principles of your association (the creative, organizational, commercial, and humane goals)

The creative (credo), very briefly--the use of good literature;
the organizational-commercial--a self-supporting theater without a permanent troupe; actors work on the basis of an agreement; the humane--a collective of people who share the same ideas.

5. How many people are in your collective today? 15

Men: 10

Women: 5

from 26 to 35: 14

from 36 to 45: 1

How many people have a theater education? 15

7. Do you have your own rehearsal space?

a) Yes, we have our own

8. What are the dimensions of the rehearsal space which you use?

100 m^2

9. By what means do you prepare decorations, costumes, props, and so forth?

b) We use what we have

d) We prepare them ourselves

10. Do you have a special permanent location for the storage of your props?

b) We do not have a special location, but use the rehearsal space or other locations

11. Do you have a permanent location for the run of a production? Yes

12. What is real capacity of your hall? 60-80

13. What is the usual attendance? 60

14. Was it necessary for you to re-equip this location?

c) We essentially had to re-equip the location

15. How many presentations did your studio give in 1989? About 250

       at your own location: about 220 productions

       at other locations

       in Leningrad: about 20 productions

       on tour: 9 productions

16. How many spectators attended productions in your studio in 1989?

Approximately 22,500 spectators

Of this number about 3,5000 spectators on tour

17. What is the average price of a ticket to a production at your theater?

At the permanent location 2.5 rubles

On tour 2.5 rubles

18. What problems did you run into as your studio came into being?

A lack of means for a quality renovation of the location.

19. What most of all worries you and alarms you at the present time?

The insufficient dimensions of the stage and spectator's area, which impedes the creative development of the theater, as well as strengthening the financial base.

20. In your opinion, how could government and societal organizations show support for you?

The presentation of a normal theater location.

21. In your opinion, what is the central problem in the life of your studio?

The point of #19.

22. In your opinion, what is the central problem in the life of contemporary Soviet theater?

A lack of talented, originally thoughtful directors.

Your address: Leningrad, ul. Gogolia
Telephone: 312-53-52

QUESTIONNAIRES 163

The Theater of Real Art (Театр реального искусства)
3/7/90

1. When was your collective officially registered in accordance with the regulations for theater-studios?

July 1988

2. When was your first production performed?

September 1988

At which institution was your theater-studio registered?

a) The Culture Administration

In what capacity did you exist prior to registration?

As a theater-studio at Litfond which was not legally registered.

3. Name the productions in your repertoire:

N. West adapt. of E. Goroshevskii	Goroshevskii	*The Mourners' Girlfriend*
A. Bitov (*The Garden*)	Goroshevskii	*3 Photos of Monakhov's Life*
A. Popov	Goroshevskii	*The Threshold*
M. de Unamuno, F. G. Lorca, Borges	Goroshevskii	*The Demon's Game*

4. If possible, please formulate the creative credo of your studio and the principles of your association (the creative, organizational, commercial, and humane goals)

A creative credo as a basis, but also some humanity, and naturally, commercial aspects, otherwise we cannot survive.

5. How many people are in your collective today? 40

Men: 15

Women: 25

younger than 25 years: 5

from 26 to 35: 25

from 36 to 45: 10

How many people have a theater education? 20

6. What are the average earnings of the actors in your studio?

On an average 150 rubles.

7. Do you have your own rehearsal space?

a) Yes, we have our own

8. What are the dimensions of the rehearsal space which you use?

120

9. By what means do you prepare decorations, costumes, props, and so forth?

d) We prepare them ourselves

10. Do you have a special permanent location for the storage of your props?

a) Yes

11. Do you have a permanent location for the run of a production?

Yes, a rented one.

12. What is real capacity of your hall? 300

13. What is the usual attendance? 150

14. Was it necessary for you to re-equip this location?

a) No, no work was done, but we intend to.

What was accommodated at your location before it was given to the theater?

A house with apartments.

15. How many presentations did your studio give in 1989? 120 productions

    at your own location: 120 productions

16. How many spectators attended productions in your studio in 1989?

Approximately 6,000 spectators

17. What is the average price of a ticket to a production at your theater?

At the permanent location 2.4 rubles

18. What problems did you run into as your studio came into being?

1. The lack of a hall
2. The lack of means
3. The lack of documents according to which one should work
4. The instability of legislation
5. The lack of interest from competent organizations to solve problems

19. What most of all worries you and alarms you at the present time?

The political environment of the country, the economic problems which have not been solved, and, as a result, the lack of spectator interest for the theater in general.

20. In your opinion, how could government and societal organizations show support for you?

1. With means and equipment
2. With a location and advertising

21. In your opinion, what is the central problem in the life of your studio?

The uncertainty of our situation provoked by the instability of the environment in the country as a whole. The lack of sponsors.

22. In your opinion, what is the central problem in the life of contemporary Soviet theater?

The lack of means and the possibility to develop the given creative potential.

Your address: 191194 Leningrad, pr. Chernyshevskogo, d. 3, "Teatr real'nogo iskusstva"

St. Petersburg (Санкт-Петербург)

1. When was your collective officially registered in accordance with the regulations for theater-studios?

March 1989

2. When was your first production performed?

March 5, 1989

At which institution was your theater-studio registered?

a) The Culture Administration

In what capacity did you exist prior to registration?

Uncoordinated

3. Name the productions in your repertoire:

Edward Albee	Bill Reiten	*Zoo Story*
M. Iu. Lermontov	Oleg Levakov	*Two Brothers*
A. Bilibin and Chenarov	A. K. Chernozemov	*Petersburg Adultery*
Harold Pinter	O. Levakov	*Betrayal*
Jean Cocteau	A. Dalin	*Les monstres sacrés*

4. If possible, please formulate the creative credo of your studio and the principles of your association (the creative, organizational, commercial, and humane goals)

The rebirth of the classic St. Petersburg theater traditions based on the best of world and Russian literature. The creative principles of association.

5. How many people are in your collective today? 16 (with staff personnel)

Men: 9

Women: 7

younger than 25 years: 3

from 26 to 35: 10

from 36 to 45: 3

How many people have a theater education? 12

6. What are the average earnings of the actors in your studio?

On an average 180 rubles.

7. Do you have your own rehearsal space?

c) No, we have to rehearse wherever we can

9. By what means do you prepare decorations, costumes, props, and so forth?

a) We order them from an artistic staging complex

10. Do you have a special permanent location for the storage of your props?

b) We do not have a special location, but use the rehearsal space or other locations

11. Do you have a permanent location for the run of a production? No

15. How many presentations did your studio give in 1989? 130 productions

        in Leningrad: 30 productions

        on tour: 100 productions

16. How many spectators attended productions in your studio in 1989?

Approximately 26,000 spectators

Of this number 20,000 spectators on tour

17. What is the average price of a ticket to a production at your theater?

At the permanent location 2.50 rubles

On tour 3 rubles

18. What problems did you run into as your studio came into being?

The location; administrative personnel

19. What most of all worries you and alarms you at the present time?

We do not have our own home.

20. In your opinion, how could government and societal organizations show support for you?

A subsidy, the location--our own residence.

21. In your opinion, what is the central problem in the life of your studio?

The running of the productions.

22. In your opinion, what is the central problem in the life of contemporary Soviet theater?

Not to hinder work; complete independence.

QUESTIONNAIRES

7-77
4/2/90

1. When was your collective officially registered in accordance with the regulations for theater-studios?

September 1987

2. When was your first production performed?

October 1987

At which institution was your theater-studio registered?

d) At the present time the theater is the creative core of the Art Center of the Leningrad Revival Fund (Petrogradskii District).

In what capacity did you exist prior to registration?

A self-supporting brigade of the May 1 Palace of Culture

3. Name the productions in your repertoire:

J. Rodari	K. I. Filinov	*Tales on the Telephone*
S. Prokof'ev, G. Saphir	K. I. Filinov	*Puss-in-Boots*
K. I. Filinov based on Soviet classics	K. I. Filinov	*Feed Your Souls*
Saint-Exupe´ry	K. I. Filinov	*The Little Prince*
Iu. Daniel	K. I. Filinov	*Redemption*

4. If possible, please formulate the creative credo of your studio and the principles of your association (the creative, organizational, commercial, and humane goals)

A maximum of spiritual influence, a virtuoso craftsmanship, a diversity of artistic forms, a partnership

5. How many people are in your collective today? 15

Men: 10

Women: 5

younger than 25 years: 3

from 26 to 35: 8

from 36 to 45: 3

from 46 to 55: 1

How many people have a theater education? 12

6. What are the average earnings of the actors in your studio?

On an average 200 rubles.

7. Do you have your own rehearsal space?

a) Yes, we have our own

8. What are the dimensions of the rehearsal space which you use?

100 m^2

9. By what means do you prepare decorations, costumes, props, and so forth?

d) We prepare them ourselves

10. Do you have a special permanent location for the storage of your props?

a) Yes

11. Do you have a permanent location for the run of a production? Yes

12. What is real capacity of your hall? 220

13. What is the usual attendance? 200

14. Was it necessary for you to re-equip this location?

c) We essentially had to re-equip the location

What was accommodated at your location before it was given to the theater?

An assembly hall of a professional-technical school

15. How many presentations did your studio give in 1989? 162 productions

    at other locations

    in Leningrad: 142 productions

    on tour: 20 productions

16. How many spectators attended productions in your studio in 1989?

Approximately 25,000 spectators

Of this number 5,000 spectators on tour

17. What is the average price of a ticket to a production at your theater?

At the permanent location 2 rubles

On tour 3 rubles

18. What problems did you run into as your studio came into being?

Run [of a production] or hire. The lack of a permanent establishment. The need to retrain the actors.

19. What most of all worries you and alarms you at the present time?

The speed of work. Insufficient mobility.

20. In your opinion, how could government and societal organizations show support for you?

The Leningrad Revival Fund provides us with necessary and sufficient help.

21. In your opinion, what is the central problem in the life of your studio?

Small creativity and a lot of obtuse soldier's execution of orders.

22. In your opinion, what is the central problem in the life of contemporary Soviet theater?

The stereotypes of Socialist Realism which still remain, with rare exceptions, in the consciousness of the Soviet theater people.

Your address: Leningrad, Sofiiskaia ul. d. 21

QUESTIONNAIRES

The Kinematic Theater Sharmanka (Шарманка)
2/10/90

1. When was your collective officially registered in accordance with the regulations for theater-studios?

December 1989

2. When was your first production performed?

December 1989

At which institution was your theater-studio registered?

A Department of Culture of the Moscow Regional Council in Leningrad

In what capacity did you exist prior to registration?

Kinematic sculptures characteristic of theater in the home of the author Eduard Bersudskii, the actors and director in the troupe of the people's theater-studio, 4 Little Windows.

3. Name the productions in your repertoire:

S. Beckett	T. Zhakovskaia	*Endgame*
T. Pogorel'skaia	T. Zhakovskaia	*The Wheel*

4. If possible, please formulate the creative credo of your studio and the principles of your association (the creative, organizational, commercial, and humane goals)

The symbiosis of kinematic sculpture, of the dramatic actor, of the actor in a mask, of the actor with puppets and further experiments in this direction.
Economically: Financial self-support with support from the Raiispolkom
In terms of membership: A team of the Ark (in the sense of a ship preserving treasures).

5. How many people are in your collective today? 7

Men: 4

Women: 3

younger than 25 years: 2

from 26 to 35: 2

from 36 to 45: 2

from 46 to 55: 1

How many people have a theater education? 1

6. What are the average earnings of the actors in your studio?

On an average 120 rubles.

7. Do you have your own rehearsal space?

a) Yes, we have our own

8. What are the dimensions of the rehearsal space which you use?

72+24 m^2

9. By what means do you prepare decorations, costumes, props, and so forth?

d) We prepare them ourselves

10. Do you have a special permanent location for the storage of your props?

a) Yes

11. Do you have a permanent location for the run of a production? Yes

12. What is real capacity of your hall? 70

13. What is the usual attendance? From 40 to 100

14. Was it necessary for you to re-equip this location?

c) We essentially had to re-equip the location

What was accommodated at your location before it was given to the theater?

It was a kindergarten.

15. How many presentations did your studio give in 1989?

       1 + 50 from January-February 1990

       at your own location: <u>all</u> productions

16. How many spectators attended productions in your studio in 1989?

Approximately 50 spectators; in 1990, 1000.

17. What is the average price of a ticket to a production at your theater?

At the permanent location 1.5 rubles

18. What problems did you run into as your studio came into being?

The deficit of building material, wiring to equip the theater, especially the lighting apparatus.

19. What most of all worries you and alarms you at the present time?

The prospect of further ruin in the country, and may God forbid, civil war and pogroms against Jews. The kinematic sculptures--these are delicate things which are easily susceptible to fire.

20. In your opinion, how could government and societal organizations show support for you?

In the organization and material guarantee of foreign tours (packing, transportation, and insurance).

21. In your opinion, what is the central problem in the life of your studio?

Wiring and electrical apparatuses are needed, the strengthening of the actor's training and the technical possibilities for the creation of new kinematic sculptures.

22. In your opinion, what is the central problem in the life of contemporary Soviet theater?

This is a Gordian knot.

Your address: Leningrad, Moskovskii pr., d. 151 "A"
Telephone: 297-26-66

The Dark Blue Bridge (Синий мост)
2/7/90

1. When was your collective officially registered in accordance with the regulations for theater-studios?

May 1987

2. When was your first production performed?

May 1987

At which institution was your theater-studio registered?

d) The Union of Light Textile Industry

In what capacity did you exist prior to registration?

Basement (underground) enthusiasts.

3. Name the productions in your repertoire:

L. Andreev	M. Grif	*A Horse in the Senate*
P. Mérimée	M. Grif	*The Temptation of Saint Anthony*
N. Nekrasov	M. Grif	*Autumn Boredom*
L. Zorin	V. Markov	*Carnival*

4. If possible, please formulate the creative credo of your studio and the principles of your association (the creative, organizational, commercial, and humane goals)

Petty or small malice, greater than all that is the best in us.

5. How many people are in your collective today? 24

Men: 13

Women: 11

younger than 25 years: 10

from 26 to 35: 14

How many people have a theater education? 2

6. What are the average earnings of the actors in your studio?

On an average 180 rubles.

7. Do you have your own rehearsal space?

b) No, we rent a permanent location

8. What are the dimensions of the rehearsal space which you use?

80 m^2

9. By what means do you prepare decorations, costumes, props, and so forth?

b) We use what we have

d) We prepare them ourselves

10. Do you have a special permanent location for the storage of your props?

b) We do not have a special location, but use the rehearsal space other locations

11. Do you have a permanent location for the run of a production? Yes

12. What is real capacity of your hall? 60

13. What is the usual attendance? 30-40

14. Was it necessary for you to re-equip this location?

c) We essentially had to re-equip the location

What was accommodated at your location before it was given to the theater?

The whole Palace of Culture was by itself and our location was a part of it.

15. How many presentations did your studio give in 1989? 10 productions

       at your own location: 10 productions

16. How many spectators attended productions in your studio in 1989?

Approximately 300-400 spectators

17. What is the average price of a ticket to a production at your theater?

At the permanent location 1 ruble

18. What problems did you run into as your studio came into being?

Soviet power and a loss of enthusiasm. There is a greater number of (girls) actresses than actors.

19. What most of all worries you and alarms you at the present time?

The ranks are thinning.

20. In your opinion, how could government and societal organizations show support for you?

Financially and with advertising.

21. In your opinion, what is the central problem in the life of your studio?

The personal life, difficulties in the everyday lives of the participants.

22. In your opinion, what is the central problem in the life of contemporary Soviet theater?

The theater, and not for the first time, has reached the point where there is no drama conforming to the ideas, and more importantly, to the aesthetic demands of the stage.

Your address: Leningrad, per. Antonenko d. 2, DK Volodarskogo
Telephone: 314-05-51

Sabbath (Суббота)
2/19/90

1. When was your collective officially registered in accordance with the regulations for theater-studios?

January 19, 1990

2. When was your first production performed?

March 18, 1969

At which institution was your theater-studio registered?

d) At the Fruzenskii Ispolkom of the Council of Workers' Deputies in Leningrad

In what capacity did you exist prior to registration?

1969-1978 -a theater club (in the system of unions)
1978-1986 -a people's theater (in the system of unions)
1987-1989 -a theater functioning on financial self-support
1990 -a theater studio in the State system

3. Name the productions in your repertoire:

Smirnov-Nesvitskii (Author)	*Windows, Streets, and Near the Gateways*
	Five Corners
	Kozlova and Kuritsyna
	The Circle Adapted for the Stage
	The Suicide
adapt. of E. M. Remark	*Three Comrades*
	Peasant Actors
	The Stop Lever
adapt. of Shakespeare	*Who is Bleeding? (Macbeth)*

*All productions are directed by Smirnov-Nesvitskii. He is the author of all of the plays except for *The Suicide* by Erdman and S. Mogilevskaia's *Peasant Actors*.

4. If possible, please formulate the creative credo of your studio and the principles of your association (the creative, organizational, commercial, and humane goals)

A theater club with the participation of professional and non-professional actors, with the aesthetics of the hall where the actors include the audience in the performance, a repertoire, arising from the mutual life of the collective; original scenarios; and the motto: "About Yourself, According to One's Own; We Perform for Our Following."

5. How many people are in your collective today?

younger than 25 years: 24

from 26 to 35: 6

from 36 to 45: 6

from 46 to 55: 4

older than 56: 4

How many people have a theater education? 6

6. What are the average earnings of the actors in your studio?

On an average 120 rubles.

7. Do you have your own rehearsal space?

a) Yes, we have our own

8. What are the dimensions of the rehearsal space which you use?

200 m^2

9. By what means do you prepare decorations, costumes, props, and so forth?

d) We prepare them ourselves

10. Do you have a special permanent location for the storage of your props?

a) Yes

11. Do you have a permanent location for the run of a production? Yes

12. What is real capacity of your hall? 100

13. What is the usual attendance? 100

14. Was it necessary for you to re-equip this location?

b) Cosmetic work was done

What was accommodated at your location before it was given to the theater?

Small groups of the Palace of Culture.

15. How many presentations did your studio give in 1989? 132 productions

at your own location: 101 productions

at other locations: 31

in Leningrad: 112 productions

on tour: 20 productions

16. How many spectators attended productions in your studio in 1989?

Approximately 15,000 spectators

Of this number 4,000 spectators on tour

17. What is the average price of a ticket to a production at your theater?

At the permanent location 1.5 rubles

On tour 1.5 rubles

18. What problems did you run into as your studio came into being?

The absence of State subsidies, a bad location, the absence of a means to advertise, difficulties with the distribution of tickets, difficulties with the formation of a disciplined collective.

19. What most of all worries you and alarms you at the present time?

The general crisis in theatrical art, the attack on the theater by mass spectacles (media) which is reflected in attendance.

20. In your opinion, how could government and societal organizations show support for you?

The introduction of taxes on government organizations, cooperatives, and so forth for the benefit of the theater studio movement, to allot a new suitable location in the center of the town.

21. In your opinion, what is the central problem in the life of your studio?

Maintaining a hold on a loyal following of spectators, filling up the hall [a full house], the perfection of the actors' mastery, discipline in the collective.

22. In your opinion, what is the central problem in the life of contemporary Soviet theater?

A way-out from the crisis [of the theater], a return of society's, the spectators' attention

Studio-87 (Студия-87)

1. When was your collective officially registered in accordance with the regulations for theater-studios?

June 25, 1987

2. When was your first production performed?

August 1, 1987

At which institution was your theater-studio registered?

a) The Culture Administration and the Museum-Preserve in the town of Pushkin

In what capacity did you exist prior to registration?

A collective existed which consisted of unemployed professional actors

3. Name the productions in your repertoire:

Iu. Kariakin	Malyshchitskii	*The Endless Lyceum*
A. Volodin	Malyshchitskii	*Dialogues*
B. Goller	Malyshchitskii	*One Hundred Bestuzhev Brothers*
Collectively	Malyshchitskii	*Act with Us*
Poetry-Song	Malyshchitskii	*Get Acquainted, It's Us*
V. Vysotskii	Malyshchitskii	*The Way I am Gazing Today*
Pasternak, Mandel'shtam, etc.	Malyshchitskii	*The Cutting Edge of Life*

4. If possible, please formulate the creative credo of your studio and the principles of your association (the creative, organizational, commercial, and humane goals)

*The questionnaire was completed directly before a performance. There was not enough time to complete this question.

5. How many people are in your collective today? 21

Men: 16

Women: 5

younger than 25 years: 6

from 26 to 35: 8

from 36 to 45: 3

How many people have a theater education? 21

6. What are the average earnings of the actors in your studio?

On an average 200 rubles.

7. Do you have your own rehearsal space?

a) Yes, we have our own

8. What are the dimensions of the rehearsal space which you use?

180 m^2

9. By what means do you prepare decorations, costumes, props, and so forth?

a) We order them from an artistic staging complex

10. Do you have a special permanent location for the storage of your props?

a) Yes

11. Do you have a permanent location for the run of a production? Yes

12. What is real capacity of your hall? 250

13. What is the usual attendance? 60

14. Was it necessary for you to re-equip this location?

c) We essentially had to re-equip the location

What was accommodated at your location before it was given to the theater?

A House of Pioneers

15. How many presentations did your studio give in 1989? 200 productions

    at your own location: 200 productions

16. How many spectators attended productions in your studio in 1989?

Approximately 20,000 spectators

17. What is the average price of a ticket to a production at your theater?

At the permanent location 2 rubles

18. What problems did you run into as your studio came into being?

Mutual relations with a sponsor, the organization of the running [of a production] for the demands of the public forced us to change our position towards commercialization.

19. What most of all worries you and alarms you at the present time?

The disharmony between the artistic goals of the theater and the directives of the sponsor

20. In your opinion, how could government and societal organizations show support for you?

If they were really interested in the development of the theater-studios, they could help us a lot. But there is no such interest.

21. In your opinion, what is the central problem in the life of your studio?

The impossibility to devote oneself to the creative process because of the enormous number of concert appearances.

22. In your opinion, what is the central problem in the life of contemporary Soviet theater?

A personal lack of interest on the part of theater people in the creative process.

Terra-Mobile (Терра-мобиле)
4/4/90

2. When was your first production performed?

April 1981

At which institution was your theater-studio registered?

b) The Youth Culture Center (Frunzenskii District)

In what capacity did you exist prior to registration?

As a studio

3. Name the productions in your repertoire:

Folklore	V. Mikheenko	*"What's the Point?"*
V. Mikheenko	V. Mikheenko	*The Flock*
V. Mikheenko	V. Mikheenko	*Captain Fracas*
Ingeborg Bachmann	V. Mikheenko	*The Good God of Manhattan*
V. Mikheenko	V. Mikheenko	*The Warning*
V. Mikheenko	V. Mikheenko	*Shostokovich's 7th Symphony*
Max Frisch	V. Mikheenko	*I Imagine...*
V. Mikheenko	V. Mikheenko	*The Personal Life*

4. If possible, please formulate the creative credo of your studio and the principles of your association (the creative, organizational, commercial, and humane goals)

The credo suggested on the poster--principles of a union on the basis of creativity

5. How many people are in your collective today? 16

Men: 9

Women: 7

younger than 25 years: 7

from 26 to 35: 7

from 36 to 45: 2

7. Do you have your own rehearsal space?

b) No, we rent a permanent location

8. What are the dimensions of the rehearsal space which you use?

35 m²

9. By what means do you prepare decorations, costumes, props, and so forth?

b) We use what we have

d) We prepare them ourselves

10. Do you have a special permanent location for the storage of your props?

b) We do not have a special location, but use the rehearsal space or other locations

11. Do you have a permanent location for the run of a production? No

What was accommodated at your location before it was given to the theater?

An auxiliary work location

15. How many presentations did your studio give in 1989? 204 productions

        at other locations

        in Leningrad: 81 productions

        on tour: 123 productions

16. How many spectators attended productions in your studio in 1989?

Approximately 60,000 spectators

Of this number 40,000 spectators on tour

17. What is the average price of a ticket to a production at your theater?

At the permanent location 2 rubles

On tour 2.5-5 rubles

18. What problems did you run into as your studio came into being?

Administrative problems
Advertising
Financial problems

19. What most of all worries you and alarms you at the present time?

The environment in the country

20. In your opinion, how could government and societal organizations show support for you?

The abolition of censorship
The permission to work in the street (Officially we are prevented from working in the street)

21. In your opinion, what is the central problem in the life of your studio?

The desire to be understood

The House on Trinity Meadow (Дом на Троицком поле)

1. When was your collective officially registered in accordance with the regulations for theater-studios?

September 1989

2. When was your first production performed?

September 1989

At which institution was your theater-studio registered?

d) Founder: The Culture Section of the Nevsky Ispolkom at the Lenin Palace of Culture

In what capacity did you exist prior to registration?

An amateur people's theater-studio

3. Name the productions in your repertoire:

M. Gorky adapt. A. Maslov	A. Maslov	*Strasti-mordasti*
Doctor Seuss libretto V. Maslova	V. Maslova	*Fairy Tales about Horton the Elephant*
V. Maslova	V. Maslova	*Who are you?*

4. If possible, please formulate the creative credo of your studio and the principles of your association (the creative, organizational, commercial, and humane goals)

A union of the actor and director as artists who enjoy full rights. From this is the principle of an association as a mutual demand on each other to search for new forms to express old truths.

5. How many people are in your collective today? 22

Men: 12

Women: 10

younger than 25 years: 20

from 26 to 35: 1

from 36 to 45: 1

How many people have a theater education? 1

6. What are the average earnings of the actors in your studio?

On an average 100 rubles.

7. Do you have your own rehearsal space?

a) Yes, we have our own

8. What are the dimensions of the rehearsal space which you use?

60 m^2

9. By what means do you prepare decorations, costumes, props, and so forth?

d) We prepare them ourselves

10. Do you have a special permanent location for the storage of your props?

a) Yes

11. Do you have a permanent location for the run of a production? Yes

12. What is real capacity of your hall? 60

13. What is the usual attendance? 60-90

14. Was it necessary for you to re-equip this location?

c) We essentially had to re-equip the location

What was accommodated at your location before it was given to the theater?

The Juvenile Military-Patriotic Club "The Seagull"

15. How many presentations did your studio give in 1989? 121 productions

       at your own location: 100 productions

       at other locations

       in Leningrad: 20 productions

       on tour: 1 production

16. How many spectators attended productions in your studio in 1989?

Approximately 2700 spectators

Of this number 500 spectators on tour

17. What is the average price of a ticket to a production at your theater?

At the permanent location 1.5 rubles

On tour 2 rubles

18. What problems did you run into as your studio came into being?

1. The financial problem
2. Difficulties in the acquisition of theater props
3. Advertising
4. Ticket sales

19. What most of all worries you and alarms you at the present time?

1. The economic survival of the studio
2. The material-technical base

20. In your opinion, how could government and societal organizations show support for you?

1. In the finance of the theater's work
2. In advertising
3. In the construction of a new theater

21. In your opinion, what is the central problem in the life of your studio?

1. The formulation of a stable creative team, capable of working on complicated creative tasks.
2. A lack of a material-technical base

22. In your opinion, what is the central problem in the life of contemporary Soviet theater?

A fundamental tearing off of contemporary theater from immemorial Russian theater traditions. The fall of theater culture. Commercialization instead of art.

Your address: Leningrad 193012, 3-ii Rabfakovskii per., dom 4, Dom na Troitskom pole

Time (Время)

1. When was your collective officially registered in accordance with the regulations for theater-studios?

August 1989

2. When was your first production performed?

January 1985

At which institution was your theater-studio registered?

d) The Leningrad Branch VTPO "Soiuzteatr"

In what capacity did you exist prior to registration?

A student theater at the Department of the Polytechnic Institute; an amateur theater at the "Scholars' Home" and so on.

3. Name the productions in your repertoire:

Herman Hesse	V. Maksimov	*Klein and Wagner*
Igor' Terent'ev	V. Maksimov	*Iordano Bruno*
M. Gelderodes	V. Maksimov	*Escorial*
Opera by Pergolesi (lib. Kuzmin)	P. Dmitriev	*Servant-Lady*

4. If possible, please formulate the creative credo of your studio and the principles of your association (the creative, organizational, commercial, and humane goals)

The creative task: the practical study of theater systems on the basis of preliminary all-round research; the creation of productions which embody a definite theater conception, for example, stage futurism, the system of A. Artaud and so on.

5. How many people are in your collective today? 16

Men: 8

Women: 8

younger than 25 years: 9

from 26 to 35: 5

from 36 to 45: 2

How many people have a theater education? 5

7. Do you have your own rehearsal space?

d) No, we rent for short periods of time

9. By what means do you prepare decorations, costumes, props, and so forth?

d) We prepare them ourselves

10. Do you have a special permanent location for the storage of your props?

c) No, the props are kept in the apartments of the studio members

11. Do you have a permanent location for the run of a production? No

15. How many presentations did your studio give in 1989? 14 productions

> at other locations
>
> in Leningrad: 14 productions

16. How many spectators attended productions in your studio in 1989?

Approximately 1,400 spectators

17. What is the average price of a ticket to a production at your theater?

At the permanent location 1-2 rubles

18. What problems did you run into as your studio came into being?

1. The lack of sources of revenue
2. The lack of status, difficulties in acquiring it
3. The lack of a location
4. Derivatives of these three
5. Censorship

19. What most of all worries you and alarms you at the present time?

1. The lack of a source of revenue
2. The impossibility to pay for the actors' work
3. The competition with commercial theater in the cultural development of the public

20. In your opinion, how could government and societal organizations show support for you?

1. The possibility for the rent-free showing of productions
2. Advertising
3. Financial help

21. In your opinion, what is the central problem in the life of your studio?

1. The contradiction of the creative and financial problems
2. The dependence on the public and the unacceptability of commercialized art
3. The necessity of the professionalization of the theater and the danger of professionalization

22. In your opinion, what is the central problem in the life of contemporary Soviet theater?

1. The commercialization of the theater, the lack of an experimental theater independent from the market.
2. The subjectivism of the "director's theater," the arbitrariness of the director
3. The complete lack of a new drama; the submission of drama to the word

QUESTIONNAIRES

The Theater Studios (Театральные мастерские)

1. When was your collective officially registered in accordance with the regulations for theater-studios?

April 1988

2. When was your first production performed?

June 1988

At which institution was your theater-studio registered

d) VOTM

In what capacity did you exist prior to registration?

As actors of various theaters

3. Name the productions in your repertoire:

L. Petrushevskaia	K. Dateshidze	*The Uncooked Leg*
N. Erdman	K. Dateshidze	*The Suicide*
A. Volodin	K. Dateshidze	*The Mother of Jesus*
Iu. Kim	K. Dateshidze	*Moscow Kitchens*

4. If possible, please formulate the creative credo of your studio and the principles of your association (the creative, organizational, commercial, and humane goals)

We have tried to create a collective of like-minded people to cherish their theater where they would be able to talk about the things troubling us today.

5. How many people are in your collective today? 16

Men: 9

Women: 7

younger than 25 years: 4

from 26 to 35: 10

from 36 to 45: 2

How many people have a theater education? 16

6. What are the average earnings of the actors in your studio?

On an average 160 rubles.

7. Do you have your own rehearsal space?

c) No, we have to rehearse wherever we can

8. What are the dimensions of the rehearsal space which you use?

9. By what means do you prepare decorations, costumes, props, and so forth?

a) We order them from an artistic staging complex

10. Do you have a special permanent location for the storage of your props?

a) Yes

11. Do you have a permanent location for the run of a production? No

15. How many presentations did your studio give in 1989? 35 productions

        in Leningrad: 27 productions

        on tour: 8 productions

16. How many spectators attended productions in your studio in 1989?

Approximately 4,273 spectators

Of this number 626 spectators on tour

17. What is the average price of a ticket to a production at your theater?

At the permanent location 2 rubles

On tour 2.5 rubles

18. What problems did you run into as your studio came into being?

Insufficient material guarantees and the actors' as well as the service staff's lack of a high level of professionalism.

19. What most of all worries you and alarms you at the present time?

The eventual fate of our collective.

20. In your opinion, how could government and societal organizations show support for you?

Necessary financial support. The theater cannot exist without subsidies.

21. In your opinion, what is the central problem in the life of your studio?

To preserve the collective despite difficult outside conditions.

22. In your opinion, what is the central problem in the life of contemporary Soviet theater?

It is important to know what to say to the audience. Find your repertoire and style and then you will find your audience.

QUESTIONNAIRES

The Crossroads (Перекресток)
3/16/90

1. When was your collective officially registered in accordance with the regulations for theater-studios?

1979

2. When was your first production performed?

1980

At which institution was your theater-studio registered?

d) The First Five-Year Plan Palace of Culture and Technology

In what capacity did you exist prior to registration?

Since 1947, as a people's theater-studio

3. Name the productions in your repertoire:

W. Shakespeare, A. Obraztsov	V. Fel'shtinskii	*Etudes about Hamlet*
M. Gruzdov	M. Gruzdov	*The Love and Life of Edith Piaff*
N. Sadur	M. Gruzdov	*The Nose*

4. If possible, please formulate the creative credo of your studio and the principles of your association (the creative, organizational, commercial, and humane goals)

Richness in content, expressiveness, intimacy

5. How many people are in your collective today? 45

Men: 25

Women: 20

How many people have a theater education? 5

7. Do you have your own rehearsal space?

a) Yes, we have our own: First Five-Year Plan Palace of Culture

9. By what means do you prepare decorations, costumes, props, and so forth?

a) We order them from an artistic staging complex

b) We use what we have

d) We prepare them ourselves

10. Do you have a special permanent location for the storage of your props?

b) We do not have a special location, but use the rehearsal space or other locations

11. Do you have a permanent location for the run of a production? Yes

12. What is real capacity of your hall? 250

13. What is the usual attendance? 200

14. Was it necessary for you to re-equip this location?

c) We essentially had to re-equip the location

What was accommodated at your location before it was given to the theater?

A hall, class

15. How many presentations did your studio give in 1989? About 80

   at other locations

   on tour: 4 productions

17. What is the average price of a ticket to a production at your theater?

At the permanent location the price is 1.5 rubles

18. What problems did you run into as your studio came into being?

Many

19. What most of all worries you and alarms you at the present time?

The quality of [the acting] craft

20. In your opinion, how could government and societal organizations show support for you?

With money

21. In your opinion, what is the central problem in the life of your studio?

Stability in the treatment of the theater as a sect

22. In your opinion, what is the central problem in the life of contemporary Soviet theater?

The treatment of it

Your address: Dekabristov, 34
Telephone: 114-20-27

PART III

THE THEATER-STUDIOS OF LENINGRAD

The Leningrad Theater-Studios: Variety, Concert, Music, and Other Studios

Leningrad Theater-Studios

1. The Fourth Wall
   Art. Dir. Vadim Zhuk
   Founder - The Theater Museum
   Ostrovsky Square, 6

2. Studio-87
   Art. Dir. V. Malyshchitskii
   Founder - The National Park Museum in the Town of Pushkin

3. Time
   Founder - The Association "Lenconcert"

4. The Young Theater
   Art. Dir. S. Spivak
   Founder - The Association "Lenconcert"

5. Theater-Studio
   Art. Dir. A. Puzyrev
   Founder - "Soiuzteatr," The Association "Svetlana"
   M. Ul'ianova Lane, 4

6. Nevsky Prospekt
   Dir. S. I. Shimilev
   Founder - "Soiuzconcert"
   M. Ul'ianova, 4

7. The Theater of the Leningrad Polytechnic Institute (amateur)
   This theater is a member of the Association of Amateur Theaters and the Association of Leningrad Theater-Studios ("on Lesnoi")

8. The Crossroads (amateur)
   The Palace of Culture (afterwards PC) of the First Five Year Plan
   This theater is a member of the Association of Amateur Theaters and the Association of Leningrad Theater-Studios

9. Four Little Windows (amateur)
   Art. Dir. T. Zhakovskaia

THE THEATER-STUDIOS OF LENINGRAD 203

This theater is a member of the Association of Amateur Theaters and the Association of Leningrad Theater-Studios

10. Sabbath (semi-professional)
    Art. Dir. Iu. A. Smirnov-Nesvitskii
    PC of Food Industry Workers
    This theater is a member of the Association of Amateur Theaters and the Association of Leningrad Theater-Studios

11. The Theater of One Actor
    Dir. G. G. Rudenko
    Founder - The All-Russian Association of Creative Studios (VOTM) STD RSFSR
    The Fontanka Embankment, 90

12. The Theater Studios
    Art. Dir. K. L. Dateshidze
    Founder - VOTM STD RSFSR

13. House of the People
    Art. Dir. L. I. Rakhlin
    Founder - The Leningrad Music Hall
    Lenin Park, 4, The Small Hall of the Music Hall

14. Petersburg
    Art. Dir. B. I. Khmel'nitskii
    The City of Kolpino, Soviet Boulevard, 29

15. The City Gate
    Art. Dir. V. P. Egorov
    Founder - The Association "Pozitron"

16. The Salon Theater "St. Petersburg"
    Art. Dir. E. V. Lukoshkov
    Founders - The Lermontov Library and the Dzerzhinskii RAIISPOLKOM
    Liteinyi prospekt, 19

17. The Theater of Real Art
    Art. Dir. E. G. Goroshevskii
    Founder - Dzerzhinskii RAIISPOLKOM
    Chernyshevsky prospekt, 3

This theater is a member of the Association of Leningrad Theater-Studios

18. The Theater-Studio under the Direction of L. Malevannaia
    Founder - The Vasileostrovskii RAIISPOLKOM
    Srednii prospekt, VO, 55
    This theater is a member of the Association of Leningrad Theater-Studios

19. The Theater on Vasil'ev Island
    Head Dir. V. L. Vorob'ev
    Founder - The Vasileostrovskii RAIISPOLKOM
    This theater is a member of the Association of Leningrad Theater-Studios

20. The Interior Theater
    Art. Dir. N. V. Beliak
    Founder - The Single Scientific Methodological Center of People's Creativity
    Rubenshtein Street, 8

21. The Comedians
    Art. Dir. M. Levshin
    This theater is a member of the Association of Leningrad Theater-Studios

22. The House on Trinity Meadow
    Art. Dir. A. Maslov
    This theater is a member of the Association of Leningrad Theater-Studios

23. The Twelve
    Art. Dir. L. Stukalov
    Founder - The Komsomol Committee of the Association "The Kirov Factory"
    Stachek prospekt (The Avenue of Strikes), 47

24. The Theater Group Transit
    Art. Dir. A. P. Mikheenko
    Founder - The Youth Center (YC) of the Vasileostrovskii RK VLKSM
    Malyi prospekt, VO, 49

25. The Comedian's Refuge
    Art. Dir. Iu. Tomoshevskii
    Founder - YC of the October District
    Gogol Street, 16

26. The Globe
    Art. Dir. V. Poletaev
    Przheval'skii Street, 18

27. The Musical-Dramatic Studio under the Direction of L. Lichovskii
    Founder - YC of Moscow Region

28. I and Thou (amateur)
    Founder - YC "Nevsky prospekt"

29. The Theater of Drama and Comedy under the Direction of N. Travin
    Founder - YC "Nevsky prospekt"

30. Wednesday - productions for children
    Art. Dir. M. Dorofeev
    Founder - YC of the Kalinin District
    The Prospekt of the Undefeated, 74

31. 7-77
    Art. Dir. K. I. Filinov
    Founder - YC of the Petrograd District
    Street of Peace, 36

32. The Dramatic Ensemble "Arena"
    Art. Dir. V. M. Badareu
    Founder - YC of the Frunzen District
    Tambov Street, 63, PC of Railway Workers

33. The Magic Bottle
    Founder - YC "Aftermath" of the Association "Kirov District"
    Stachek prospekt, 47

34. The City
    Art. Dir. S. Kurbatova
    Founder - The Dzerzhinskii YC
    Petr Lavrov Street, 29, Room 14

35. The Wonderful Glade
    Art. Dir. L. I. Kotel'nikova, Head Dir. G. M. Shagaev
    Founder - YC of the Krasnosel'skii District
    Street of the Partisan Herman, 3

36. Fragment
    Art. Dir. V. Marchenko
    Founder - YC of the Sestroretskii District

37. Beyond the Black River
    Art. Dir. O. Mendel'son
    Founder - YC of the Primorskii District

Avant-garde Theater-Studios, Theaters of Pantomime and Eurythmics

1. Avant-garde
   Founder - The Scientific Industrial Association "Plastpolimer"

2. The Clown Mime Theater "Litsedei"
   Art. Dir. V. Polunin
   The Joint Soviet-Finnish Enterprise "Sphynx"
   The Embankment on the River Kaprivka, 45

3. The Tree
   Art. Dir. A. Adasinskii
   Founder - The Leningrad Palace of Youth (LPY)
   Professor Popov Street, 47

4. Second Reality
   Art. Dir. V. Kolesnikov
   Founder - LPY
   Professor Popov Street, 47
   This theater is a member of the Association of Leningrad Theater-Studios

5. Do-Theater
   Dir. E. Kozlov
   Founder - YC of the Vasileostrovskii District
   Malyi prospekt, VO, 49

6. The Infant of Asia
   Dir. A. Spiridonova
   Founder, address (same as #5)

7. The Musical-Plastic Theater Under the Direction of Mokrousova
   Founder - YC of the Vyborgskii District

8. Neo
   Art. Dir. Strel'nikov
   Founder - (same as #7)

9. The Theater-Studio of Pantomime
   Art. Dir. P. Efimov
   Founder - YC of the Vyborgskii District
   Karl Marx Prospekt, 75

10. The Musical-Plastic Theater-Studio
    Art. Dir. L. I. Koreneva
    Founder - (same as #9)

11. The Road
    Art. Dir. V. Koifman
    Founder - YC of the Smol'ninskii District
    Bakunin Street, 2
    This theater is a member of the Association of Leningrad Theater-Studios

12. The Experimental Theater Association "Gun-go"
    Art. Dir. S. Gogun
    Founder - YC of the Kalinin District

13. The Studio "Terra-Mobile"
    Art. Dir. V. I. Mikheenko
    Founder - YC of the Frunzen District

14. The Mime-Theater "Suggested Circumstances"
    Founder - YC "Aftermath" of the Association "The Kirov Factory"
    Stachek prospekt, 47

Puppet Theater-Studios

1. The Puppet
   Art. Dir. E. Iu Ugriumov
   Founder - The Kirov Central Park of Culture and Relaxation
   Elagin Island, 8
   This theater is a member of the Association of Leningrad Theater-Studios

2. The Wooden Horse
   The Founder - PC "Contemporary"
   The City of Pushkin

3. The Theater of Shadows "Luminary"
   The Founder - YC of the Vasileostrovskii District
   Malyi prospekt, VO, 49

4. Da-Net
   Art. Dir. B. Iu. Ponizovskii
   The Founder - YC of the Vyborg District
   Marx Prospekt, 75
   This theater is a member of the Association of Leningrad Theater-Studios

5. The Stray Dog
   Art. Dir. M. K. Prokof'eva
   Founder - YC "Nevsky prospekt"
   Nevsky prospekt, 82

6. The Magic Screen
   Art. Dir. G. M. Eguraeva
   Founder - YC "Nevsky prospekt"
   Borodinskii Street, 12 - School #308

7. The Little Mouse
   Art. Dir. D. Timofeev
   Founder - YC of the Petrodvorets District
   The City of Petrodvorets, Kalinin Street, 7

8. The Showman
   Art. Dir. I. G. Ramonokova
   Founder - YC of the October District

Przheval'skii Street, 18

Musical Theater-Studios

1. The Children's Musical Theater
   Founder - The Association "Lenconcert"

2. The Chamber Music Theater
   Founder - The Association "Lenconcert"

3. The Opera of Puppets
   Art. Dir. Lopukhin
   Founder - The Children's Fund

4. Satire
   Art. Dir. A Schastlivtsev
   Founder - YC of Vasileostrovskii District

5. The Chamber Ballet
   The Founder - YC of the October District
   Przheval'skii Street, 18

Theater-Studios of Mass Holidays, Spectacles, and Presentations

1. The Street Theater

2. The Mask

3. The Landschaft Theater

4. Children's Holidays

5, 6. Two Theater Spectacle Groups

7. The Carousel

8. The Creative Group of Night Programs

9. The Traveling Show

Variety, Concert, Literary-Musical, Ethnographic, Circus, and Like Collectives

1. The Leningrad Theater of Fashion
2. Fashion and Song
3. The Theater "Variety"
4. Premiere
5. The Night Theater
6. Secret
7. Rock
8. Planet
9. Benefit
10. The Variety "Troika"
11. The Screen
12. The Student Philharmonic of Financial Self-Support
13. Divertissement
14. Record
15. The Poesy Concert
16. Two Associations of Bards
17. Satire, Humor, Illusion
18. Old Petersburg
19. The Philharmonic Branch
20. The Theater of the Composer S. Samoilov

21. The Happy Divertissement
22. The Men'shikov Miniature Theater
23. One Person
24. The Folk Music Collective "Sprin"
25. The Show Group "Rhythms of the Planet"
26. Theater-Studio
27. The Mask
28. The Concert Program
29. The Fellowship of Literateurs
30. Background
31. The Synthesis Group "Digest"
32. The Folklore Group
33. Dixieland "Tonos" (Tone)
34. Villa Rode
35. The Association "Theater"
36. The Morozov Literary Association
37. Balalaika
38. The Association of Composers Under the Direction of Iu. Kas'iannik
39. The Epos
40. The Modus

41. Rendezvous

42. Movies and Time

43. The Literary-Musical Association of M. Zasetskaia

44. Belun

45. The Bench

46. On the Islands

47. Pioneer

48. Gauranga

49. Sakartvelo

50. The Folk Circus

51. Spring

52. Valentia

53. Office

54. The People

55. The Alternative

56. The Studio of Variety Presentations of I. Korneliuk

57. Constellation

58. Duende

   -"-"-"-

59. Petergof

60. Image

61. Reflection

62. Meetings

63. Impressario

64. Sphere

65. The Literary Association of Kalashnikova

66. Specter

67. The Advertising-Artistic Association "Synthesis"

68. Old Nevsky

69. Dialogue

70. Neo

Rock Groups

A great number of rock groups also exist (more than forty), working as theater-studios. In the majority of cases, the founders of such collectives are the youth centers of the various city districts. The most famous of them are "Auction," "The Jungle," "Television," "DDT," "The Rainy Season," and "Zero".

This actual list was composed as a senior thesis by S. A. Ostanina and is the result of research conducted by an engineer of the Department of Planning and Organization of Theater Affairs, M. A. Naimark. The thesis was defended at the Leningrad State Institute of Theater, Music, and Cinematography in June of 1989.

It is necessary to note that the majority of facts correspond to May, while additions and details were made in the fall of 1989. The theater-studios are in a constant state of flux--they arise, die, transform themselves, and thus in the course of time an actual list may not correspond to the genuine state of affairs.

Commentaries and Additions to the List of the Leningrad Theater-Studios (June-July of 1991)

2. Does not exist

4. Merged with the State theater on the Fontanka

5. No information

6. The Actor's Home is the base for this theater

8. It is not "amateur" but semi-professional
   Artistic Director - M. Gruzdov. Address: ul. Dekabristov, 34

9. The theater "Four Little Windows" has practically merged with the theater "Sharmanka"

   11 through 13 do not exist

14. Artistic Director - A. Polukhina

15. No information

19. Artistic Director - V. V. Osipov

21. The Founder - The Lenoblispolkom Culture Administration

22. Address: Sh. Rabfakovskii per., 4

23. No information

24. No information

25. Founders - City Administration; Baltic Sea Steamship Line and citizen Iu. Tomashevskii

26. It exists. Founded by the Center for Creative Work of the Kuibyshevskii District of St. Petersburg

    No information for 27 through 31

32. Semi-professional. The Directors are N. N. Pereviazko and A. S. Nikulin. The founder - The Palace of Culture of Railway Workers
    Address: Tambovskaia 63

33. No information

34. Sponsor SPMTS "October"

    No information for 35 through 37

38. Moskovskii prospekt
    The Founder - The Il'ich Palace of Culture, MTS of the Moscow District
    The Artistic Director is A. Birulia

39. The Leningrad Chamber Theater
    The Culture Section of the Smol'nyi RAIISPOLKOM
    V. Koifman
    The Theater has moved to a new address. Telephone 277-1218

40. Second Reality
    The Founder - LO VPTO "Soiuzteatr"
    The Artistic Director is V. P. Kolesnikov
    The Leningrad Palace of Youth

Avant-garde Theater-Studios, Theaters of Pantomime and Eurythmics

1. No information

4. A dramatic theater

6. Does not exist

    No information on 7 through 10

11. A dramatic theater

14. No information

15. The Theatrical-Research Laboratory under the Direction of V. Maksimov (it is gravitating toward a dramatic theater)
    The Founder - LO VPTO "Soiuzteatr"
    Address: The Polytechnic Institute

16. The Theater of the Absurd
    The Founder - MTS of the Vasileostrovskii District
    The Artistic Director is M. Gindin

Malyi pr., 49

17. Da-Net - A Place for the Dramatic Actor
Founded by the Society for the Encouragement of Modern Art
"A-Ia" The Leningrad Branch
The Artistic Director is B. Ponizovskii
ul. Pushkinskaia, 10-124

Puppet Theater-Studios

No information on 2 through 3

4. This is not a puppet theater, but avant-garde, research. Puppets and objects are used in the work

No information from 6 through to 8

The Opera of Puppets (A Musical Puppet Theater)
The Founder - The Children's Fund
The Artistic Director is V. Lopukhin
The Address: Nevsky, 60

Musical Theater-Studios

Numbers 1 and 2 are not theater-studios and never were. They are State theaters.

3. A puppet theater

4. A musical ensemble of old music

Lately the changes in our country have begun to take place with alarming speed. A month ago there were only two practical ways to create a new theater--the organization of a State theater or another with any founder--but absolutely in keeping with the approximate status of the theater-studios in 1989.

Thus, most of the present list of theaters are essentially not theater-studios. We are inclined to call them studios of alternative forms (that is, theaters, forms of an organization which are alternatives to customary State theaters).

Today the situation in the Russian Republic has, in any case, changed noticeably. Less than a month ago the resolution of the Council of

Ministers was accepted, which allows anyone to organize theaters, the country, the city, business, the private individual, foreign organizations and citizens, groups of founders, etc. A founder may not in any way interfere in the theater's activity or demand any profits. All theaters are exempt from paying taxes, except mandatory social payments and payments to authors. State and municipal theaters have budgeted financial support.

All of the aforementioned allows one to suggest that in the near future we will no longer be confronted with the prodigious flow of theater-studios. Moreover, we will not be calling new theaters alternative, because the law confirmed the existence of a variety of theater organizations in the Republic.

Ленинградские театры-студии
эстрадные, концертные, музыкальные и
прочие коллекетивы

Драматические театры-студии

1. Четвертая стена
2. Студия - 87
3. Время
4. Молодой театр
5. Театр-студия
6. Невский проспект
7. Театр Ленинградского Политехнического института
8. Перекресток
9. Четыре окошка
10. Суббота
11. Театр одного актера
12. Театральная мастерская
13. Народный дом
14. Петербург
15. Городская застава
16. Салон-театр «Санкт-Петербург»
17. Театр реального искусства
18. Театр-студия
    под руководством Л. Малеванной
19. Театр на Васильевском острове

20. Интерьерный театр
21. Комедианты
22. Дом на Троицком поле
23. Двенадцать
24. Театральная группа «Транзит»
25. Приют комедианта
26. Глобус
27. Музыкально-драматическая студия
28. Я и ты
29. Театр драмы и комедии
30. «Среда» - спектакли для детей
31. Театр 7 - 77
32. Драматический ансамбль «Арена»
33. Волшебная бутылка
34. Город
35. Чудесная поляна
36. Фрагмент
37. За черной речкой

Авангардные театры-студии, театры пантомимы и пластики

1. Авангард
2. Клоун-мим театр «Лицедеи»
3. Дерево
4. Вторая реальность
5. До-театр
6. Инфанта Азии
7. Музыкально-пластический театр
8. Нео
9. Театр-студия пантомимы
10. Музыкально-пластический театр-студия
11. Дорога
12. Экспериментальное театральное объединение «Гун-го»
13. Студия «Терра-мобиле»
14. Мим-театр «Предлагаемые обстоятельства»

Кукольные театры-студии

1. Кукла
2. Деревянная лошадь
3. Театр теней «Светило»
4. Да-нет
5. Бродячая собака
6. Волшебная ширма
7. Мышуня
8. Балаганчик

Музыкальные театры-студии

1. Детский музыкальный театр
2. Камерный музыкальный театр
3. Опера кукол
4. Сатир
5. Камерный балет

Театры-студии массовых праздников, зрелищ, представлений и т.п.

1. Уличный театр
2. Маска
3. Ландшафт-театр
4. Детские праздники
5, 6. Две театрально-зрелищные группы
7. Карусель
8. Творческая группа ночных программ
9. Балаган

Эстрадные, концертные, литературно-музыкальные, этнографические, цирковые и т.п. коллективы

1. Ленинградский театр моды
2. Мода и песня

3. Театр «Варьете»
4. Премьера
5. Ночной театр
6. Секрет
7. Рок
8. Планета
9. Бенефис
10. Варьете «Тройка»
11. Экран
12. Студенческая хозрасчетная филармония
13. Дивертисмент
14. Рекорд
15. Поэзо-концерт
16. Два объединения бардов
17. Сатира, юмор, иллюзия
18. Старый Петербург
19. Филармонический филиал
20. Театр композитора С. Самойлова
21. Веселый дивертисмент
22. Театр миниатюр Меньшикова
23. Один человек
24. Коллектив народной песни «Сприн»
25. Шоу-группа «Ритмы планеты»
26. Театр-ателье
27. Маска
28. Концертная программа
29. Товарищество литераторов
30. Фон
31. Синтез-группа «Дайджест»
32. Фольклорная группа
33. Диксиленд «Тонос»
34. Вилла Родэ
35. Объединение «Театр»
36. Литературное объединение Морозова
37. Балалайка
38. Ассоциация композиторов под. рук. Ю. Касьянника
39. Эпос
40. Модус

41. Рандеву
42. Кино и время
43. Литературно-музыкальное объединение М. Засецкой
44. Белун
45. Скамейка
46. На островах
47. Пионер
48. Гауранга
49. Сакартвело
50. Народный цирк
51. Весна
52. Валенсия
53. Офис
54. Люди
55. Альтернатива
56. Студия эстрадных представлений И. Корнелюка
57. Созвездие
58. Дуэнде
  -"-"-"
59. Петергоф
60. Образ
61. Отражение
62. Встречи
63. Импрессарио
64. Шар
65. Литературное объединение Калашниковой
66. Спектр
67. Рекаламно-художественное объединение «Синтез»
68. Староневский
69. Диалог
70. Нео

Рок-группы

Существует также большое количество (более 40) рок-групп, работающих в статусе театров-студий. В большинстве случаев учредителями таких коллективов становятся молодежные центры различных районов города.

Наиболее известные среди них: «Аукцион», «Джунгли», «Телевизор», «ДДТ», «Сезон дождей», «Ноль»...

Настоящий список составлен на основе дипломного сочинения Останиной С. А. и результатов исследования, проводимого инженером кафедры планирования и организации театрального дела Наймарк М. А. Дипломная работа защищена в Ленинградском Государственном Институте Театра, Музыки и Кинематографии в июне 1989.

Нужно отметить, что основной массив данных списка соответствует маю, а дополнения и уточнения - осени 1989 года. Театры-студии находятся в постоянном движении - возникают, умирают, трансформируются, поэтому с течением времени настоящий список может в чем-то перестать соответствовать реальному положению дел.

PHOTOGRAPHS AND ILLUSTRATIONS

Iurii Aleksandrovich Smirnov-Nesvitskii

Subbota

Aleksandr Alekseevich Maslov

PHOTOGRAPHS AND ILLUSTRATIONS 227

Dom na Troitskom pole

Tat'iana Andreevna Zhakovskaia

Sharmanka

Lev Gennad'evich Sundstrem

PHOTOGRAPHS AND ILLUSTRATIONS 231

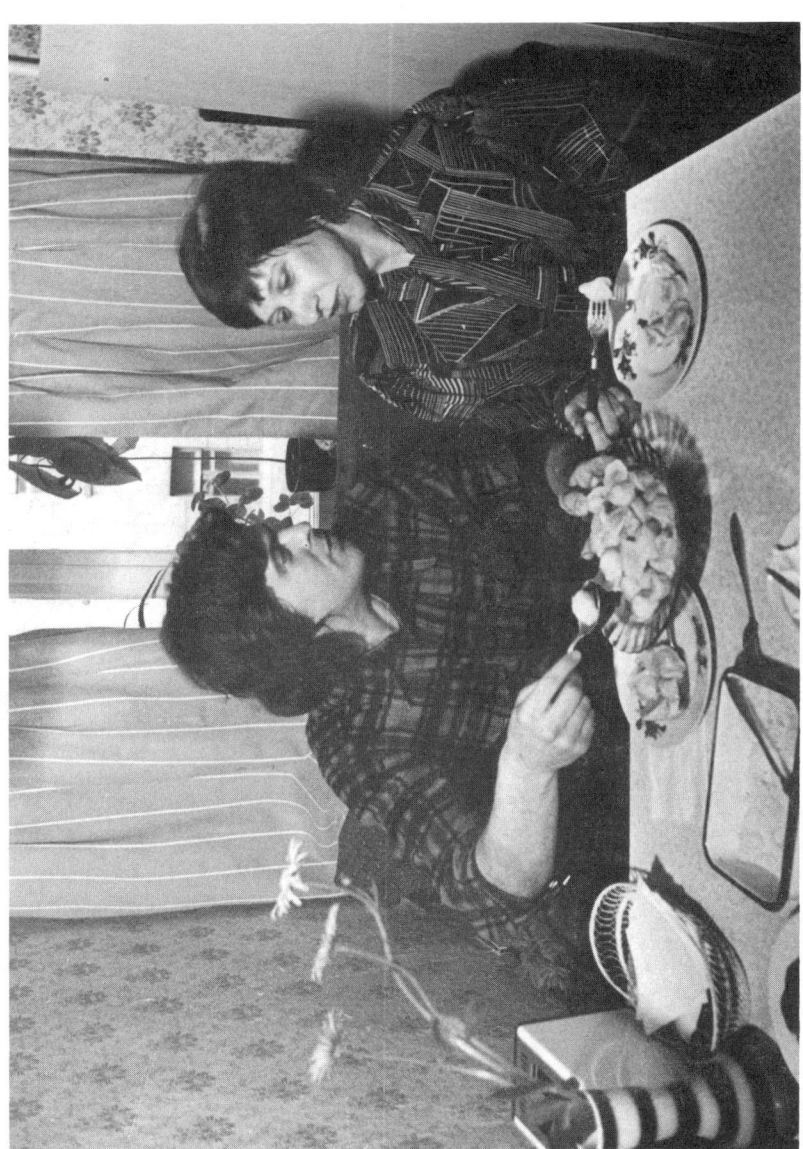

Elena Viktorovna Markova (at right) and the Author

Akhmat Rashidovich Bairamkulov

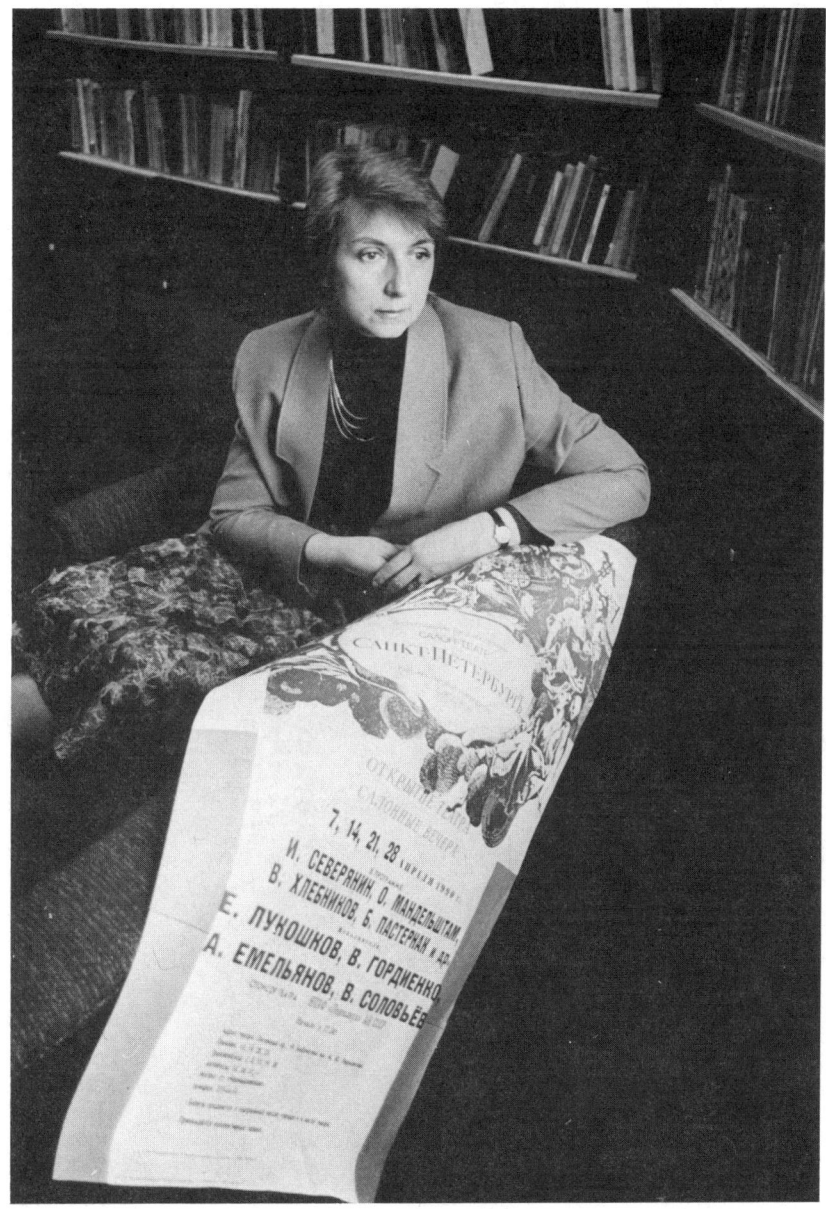

Alla Grigor'evna Minina

Vadim Zhuk

PHOTOGRAPHS AND ILLUSTRATIONS 235

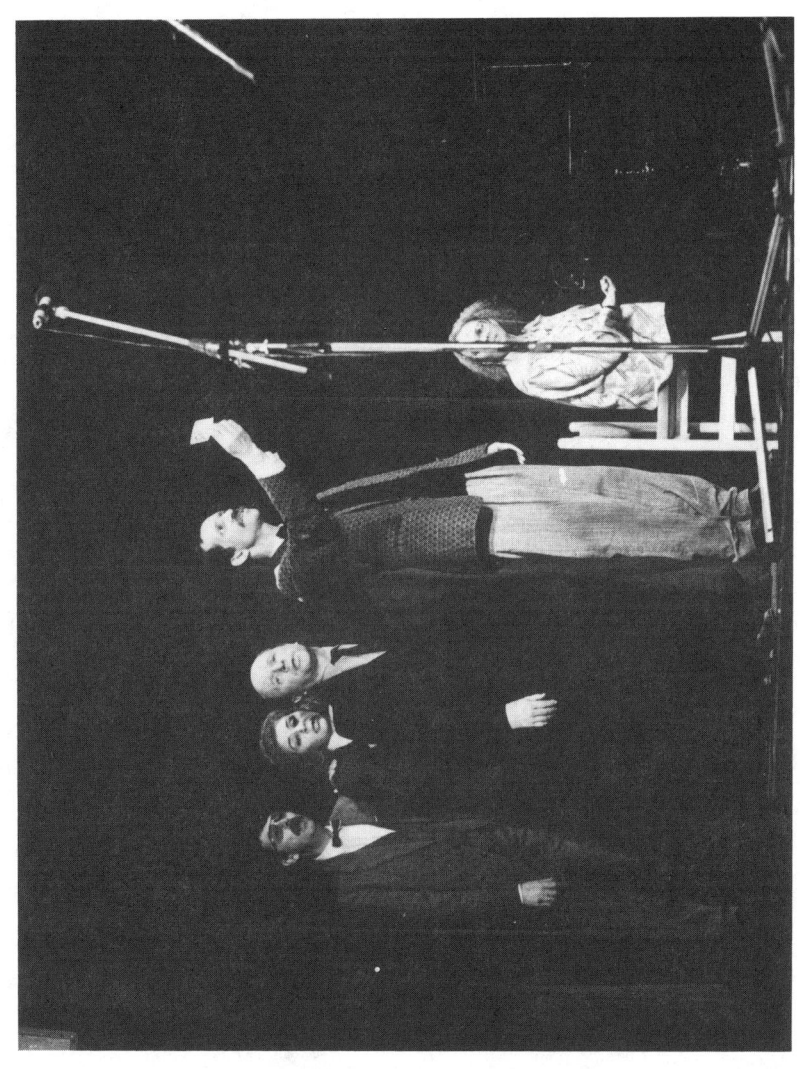

Chetvertaia stena

Marina Iur'evna Dmitrievskaia (holding journal) with the Staff of *Predstavlenie*

Program from *We Play the King*

Vladimir Bogdanov, K. N. Chernozemov, and Evgenii Ganelin

Maksim Maksimov

Isaak Romanovich Shtokband

K. N. Chernozemov, Evgenii Ganelin, and Vladimir Bogdanov

Elena Viktorovna Markova (at right) and the Author

Bibliography

Blok, Aleksandr. *Pis'ma k zhene.* Tom 89, *Literaturnoe nasledstvo.* Moskva: Nauka, 1978.

Carnicke, Sharon Marie. *The Theatrical Instinct: Nikolai Evreinov and the Russian Theatre of the Early Twentieth Century.* New York: Peter Lang, 1989.

Edwards, Paul, ed. *The Encyclopedia of Philosophy.* Vol. 3. New York: The Macmillan Company, 1967.

Efros, Anatolii. *Prodolzhenie teatral'nogo rasskaza.* Moskva: Iskusstvo, 1985.

Gladkov, Aleksandr. *Teatr: Vospominaniia i razmyshleniia.* Moskva: Iskusstvo, 1980.

Gorchakov, Nikolai. *The Vakhtangov School of Stage Art.* Moscow: Foreign Language Publishing House, 195-?.

Grotowski, Jerzy. *Towards a Poor Theatre.* New York: Simon and Schuster, 1968.

Iankovskii, M. O. *Leningradskii teatr komedii.* Leningrad: Iskusstvo, 1968.

Kelly, Kathleen White. *Jean Anouilh: An Annotated Bibliography.* Metuchen: The Scarecrow Press, 1973.

Milne, Lesley. "Mikhail Bulgakov: the Status of the Dramatist and the Status of the Text." In *Russian Theatre in the Age of Modernism*, eds. Robert Russell and Andrew Barratt, 236-259. New York: St. Martin's Press, 1990.

Rudnitskii, K. L. *Rezhisser Meierkhol'd.* Moskva: Nauka, 1968.

_____, ed. *Sovetskii teatr.* Moskva: Iskusstvo, 1967.

Sayler, Oliver M. *The Russian Theatre.* New York: Brentano's Publishers, 1922.

Slonim, Marc. *Russian Theater: From the Empire to the Soviets.* Cleveland: The World Publishing Company, 1961.

Slovar' sovremennogo russkogo literaturnogo iazyka. Tom 6. Moskva: Akademiia Nauk SSSR, 1957.

Tovstonogov, G. *Zerkalo stseny: O professii rezhissera.* Leningrad: Iskusstvo, 1980.

Vendrovskaya, Lyubov and Kaptereva, Galina. *Evgeny Vakhtangov.* Moscow: Progress Publishers, 1982.

Worral, Nick. *Modernism to Realism on the Soviet Stage.* Cambridge: Cambridge University Press, 1989.

The Contributors

Iurii Aleksandrovich Smirnov-Nesvitskii is theater critic, Doctor of Art Criticism, Director of Subbota, and author of books on Vakhtangov and Mayakovsky.

Aleksandr Alekseevich Maslov has been trained as a director. He is currently the Head Director of Dom na Troitskom pole.

Tat'iana Andreevna Zhakovskaia has worked as a theater critic and Artistic Director of Sharmanka.

Lev Gennad'evich Sundstrem was an administrator at the Leningrad State Institute of Theater, Music, and Cinematography at the time of the interview.

Elena Viktorovna Markova is a theater critic who serves as Docent of the Department of Foreign Art at the St. Petersburg State Institute of Theater, Music, and Cinematography. A Kandidat of Art Criticism, she has published extensively on theater and the arts. Her publications include three books on pantomime.

Akhmat Rashidovich Bairamkulov has been trained as a director. He is currently teaching at the St. Petersburg State Institute of Theater, Music, and Cinematography.

Alla Grigor'evna Minina is a theater critic who has worked as Editor of the journal *Iskusstvo Leningrada*.

Vadim Zhuk was trained in theater criticism. He worked for many years as a tour guide in the Leningrad State Theater Museum. He is an actor and Artistic Director of Chetvertaia stena.

Marina Iur'evna Dmitrievskaia is a theater critic who works as Docent of the Department of Russian Arts at the St. Petersburg State Institute of Theater, Music, and Cinematography. A Kandidat of Art Criticism, she regularly publishes articles on theater in journals and newspapers.

Nothing more is known about Olga Kirsanova and Dmitrii Miropol'skii.

THE CONTRIBUTORS

K. N. Chernozemov is a Laureate of the All-Russian Competition of Actors and Readers. A Kandidat of Art Criticism, he serves as the Docent of the Department of Theater Movement at the St. Petersburg State Institute of Theater, Music, and Cinematography.

Maksim Maksimov is a theater critic and Editor of the Arts Section of *Smena*.

Vadim Gushchin is a graduate of the Leningrad State Institute of Theater, Music, and Cinematography. After working at several theaters, he joined the Theater of Drama and Comedy on Liteinyi prospekt. He has worked in the United States.

Isaak Romanovich Shtokband worked as Director of the Theater Bouffe.

OHIO UNIVERSITY LIBRARY
Please return this book as soon as you have finished with it. In order to avoid a fine it must be returned by the late